Twenty-first Century Literary and Cultural Theory Renaissance

Vincent B. Leitch

GLOBALIZATION

Empire
Postcolonial Studies
Border Studies

Diaspora Studies
Multiculturalism
New American Studies

Resistance Studies
Surveillance and Security Studies
Body Studies
Cyborg Studies

INSTITUTIONAL STUDIES

Archive Studies
Professionalization Studies
Publishing Histories
Canonization Studies

Critical Pedagogy
Academic Labor Studies
Corporate University
Digital Humanities

GENRE

Electronic Literature
Religion and Literature
Popular Poetries
Pulp Fiction
Performance Studies

Narrative Studies
New History of Nov
Life Writing
Oratures
Outsider Arts

Affect Theory
Testimony
Sentimentality

AFFECT STUDIES

Trauma Studies
Memory Studies
Holocaust Studie:

POLITICAL ECONOMY

Neoliberalism
Late Capitalism
The New Economic Criticism
Patronage Studies

Subaltern Studies
Working-Class Studies
The Multitude
Debt Studies

BIOPOLITICS

Gender Studies
Disability Studies
Age Studies
Leisure Studies

POPULAR CULTURE

Celebrity Studies
Public Intellectuals
Public Sphere
Subcultures

Popular Music
Fashion Studies
Sport Studies
Gaming Studies

Sound Studies
Visual Culture Studies
TV Studies
Film Studies

MEDIA STUDIES

Book History
Periodical Studies
New Media
Social Media

RHETORIC

Literacy Studies
Discourse Analysis
Composition Studies
History of Rhetoric

Tropology
Orality
Cognitive Poetics
Reception Studies

ECOCRITICISM

Cognitive Theory
Object Studies
Technoscience Studies

Animal Studies
Food Studies
Geocriticism

New Southern U.S. Studies
Whiteness Studies
Indigenous Studies
Ethnic Studies

IDENTITY

Women's Studies
Queer Studies
Masculinity Studies
Sexuality Studies

LITERARY COMPARATIVISMS

Sinophone
Lusophone
Hispanophone
Francophone
Anglophone

Black Atlantic
Transatlantic
Transpacific
Multilingual
Translation Studies

FIGURE 1

Literary
Criticism in the
21st Century

ALSO AVAILABLE FROM BLOOMSBURY

Modern Literary Theory: A Reader, 4th Edition,
Patricia Waugh & Philip Rice
Crimes of the Future: Theory and Its Global Reproduction,
Jean-Michel Rabaté
Literary Theory: A Guide for the Perplexed, Mary Klages
*How to Read Texts: A Student Guide to Critical Approaches
and Skills, 2nd Edition*, Neil McCaw
*The Poetry Toolkit: The Essential Guide to Studying Poetry,
2nd Edition*, Rhian Williams

Literary Criticism in the 21st Century

Theory Renaissance

Vincent B. Leitch

B L O O M S B U R Y
LONDON · NEW DELHI · NEW YORK · SYDNEY

Bloomsbury Academic

An imprint of Bloomsbury Publishing Plc

50 Bedford Square	1385 Broadway
London	New York
WC1B 3DP	NY 10018
UK	USA

www.bloomsbury.com

Bloomsbury is a registered trade mark of Bloomsbury Publishing Plc

First published 2014

© Vincent B. Leitch, 2014

British Library Cataloguing-in-Publication Data
A catalogue record for this book is available from the British Library.

ISBN: PB: 978-1-4725-2770-7
HB: 978-1-4725-3252-7
ePDF: 978-1-4725-2831-5
ePub: 978-1-4725-3182-7

Library of Congress Cataloging-in-Publication Data
A catalog record for this book is available from the Library of Congress.

Typeset by Integra Software Services Pvt. Ltd.
Printed and bound in India

CONTENTS

Preface   vi

1 What I believe and why   1

2 Antitheory   11

3 The tasks of critical reading   33

4 Theory today and tomorrow   51

5 Theory crossroads   67

6 French theory's second life   91

7 Second lives of Jacques Derrida   105

8 Postmodernism revisited   121

9 Twenty-first-century theory favorites   133

10 Theory futures   151

Bibliography   159
Index   169

PREFACE

There are four major claims that I want to state at the outset. First, despite all the talk about posttheory and after theory that has been floating around for several decades, there is a theory renaissance underway. Granted, it is difficult to see at first glance. Second, as my map on the flyleaf suggests, twenty-first-century theory is knowable but unmasterable (Figure 1). This chart contains 94 subdisciplines and fields circling around 12 major topics (reminiscent of planets and satellites), which can change spheres and fuse into original combinations. Third, the twenty-first-century theory renaissance takes a characteristically postmodern form, namely disorganization or disaggregation of many subdisciplines, fields, and topics. In a world in which there are 6,800 mutual funds, 20,000 wines reviewed annually in *Wine Spectator*, and innumerable sneakers to choose from—with guides for dummies everywhere to assist us in these arcane areas—proliferation and fragmentation should come as no surprise. Fourth, the 15 or so earlier well-known twentieth-century schools and movements of theory from Marxism, psychoanalysis, and formalism to postcolonial theory, New Historicism, and queer theory are, strictly speaking, a twentieth-century phenomenon. Schools and movements do not pertain to earlier centuries of theory or to the twenty-first century. Nevertheless, they remain important today as sources and resources not only for practical literary criticism but also for teaching theory. By way of simplification, the 106 items constituting my inventory of theory can be regarded as the cultural studies movement in its disaggregated form. The take-away message of my initial set of claims is that with literary and cultural criticism today, theory, for good and ill, is everywhere and nowhere.

I anticipate several questions at this point. Is the recent transformation another victory of theory following its triumph in the 1980s? Why in any case call this complex spread "theory"? To answer the first question, I would characterize the dissemination and leveling underway as neither a triumph nor a disaster but rather a mixed blessing. Theory now occupies the role of regular practice as opposed to shocking and disruptive vanguard. Gone are the high excitement and energy revolving around theory during the cultural wars of the fin de siècle. Yet a second glance at the map, however initially befuddling, reveals that most of the current practices raise very precisely targeted critical questions of a fundamental sort. Theory, as in the past, continues to prompt and underwrite productive research and publication projects for criticism across an expanded spectrum of topics and fields. But the fractalization of theory has meant that there are very few jobs in the area. These days theory serves as an adjunct, a helpful toolkit, a secondary but indispensible strength for long-established fields and areas of literary and cultural study.

Why continue calling this proliferation "theory"? In a word, parentage. All the items on the map stem directly from recognizable contemporary schools and movements of theory. In addition, no one has successfully proposed an alternative term. I can't think of one. "Cultural studies," a likely contender, doesn't fit; it remains too amorphous, plus it lacks historical foundations and precisions of "theory." Considered comparatively, "theory" is a neutral term whereas "cultural studies" has inherited a vaguely engagé orientation linked to the social sciences. Figure 2 below offers some clarification. Here twenty-first-century theory includes distinctive methods and approaches. One among others is cultural studies.

Narrative Poetics	Quantitative Analysis
Neophenomenology	Institutional Analysis
Social Semiotics	Surface and Close Reading
New Formalisms	Histories from Below
CRITICAL APPROACHES	**CRITICAL METHODS**
Historicisms	Cultural Critique
Cultural Studies	Personal Criticism
Ethical Turn	Ethnography
Cognitive Theory	Oral History

FIGURE 2

While cultural studies and theory overlap, theory includes items not generally welcomed by cultural studies such as formalism, phenomenology, and narrative poetics, all experiencing revivals today. Although fusions abound, theory today maintains its legacy of autonomy. That said, I have nothing against, and I personally support, ongoing contemporary linkages of theory and cultural studies.

The chapters in this book follow a trajectory from statements of personal belief to return visits to key debates to recent monumentalizations of French theory to futures for theory. Chapter 1 previews the major topics, sentiments, and arguments of the book by means of a credo. It blends the professional and the personal, my work in theory and my family life, to illustrate the range of concerns pertinent to contemporary criticism. For example, the chapter dramatizes the increasingly important role during recent decades of financialization and free-market political economy as they shape family, self, and society. Here I argue for, while defining intimate critique, an adjunct to cultural critique, both of which should continue to play a central role in today's literary and cultural criticism. This chapter provides preliminary definitions of theory and postmodernism in their current versions.

Chapter 2 provides a critical account of the antitheory phenomenon that started in the 1970s and is still with us. The heterogeneous antitheory front constitutes a neglected part of the history of contemporary criticism and theory filled with contending definitions and alternative missions for theory. In exploring half a dozen exemplary indictments of theory, I develop my own critique of theory as well as clarify my own theoretical ideas and principles. In addition, I show what is at issue in the sacred antitheory oath "I love literature."

Many calls to return to close reading and renounce ideology critique have popped up in the new century. They go under various names such as uncritical, reparative, appreciative, surface, and generous reading. Chapter 3 argues against such head-in-the-sand calls. Instead it advocates and defines a program of critical reading that blends ideology critique, close reading, cultural critique (attended by intimate critique), and pleasure reading. It refuses the either/or option of close reading versus ideology critique in favor of a both/and choice suited to criticism and education in an age of intensifying class antagonisms, disruptive reconfigurations of the family, and spreading social tensions and wars.

Chapter 4 offers a challenging interview of me conducted by a prominent Chinese professor of American literature and theory teaching at Nanjing University. His outsider perspective, skeptical and informed, allows for a set of wide-ranging questions about the status nowadays of Western multiculturalism; the pertinence of New Critical formalism over against cultural studies; the situation of theory; changes to the second edition of the *Norton Anthology of Theory and Criticism* (2001, 2010); and justifications for teaching theory today. Where Chapters 1 to 3 offer declarations of my positions in argumentative contexts, Chapters 4 and 5 provide inventories of current trends and methods through dialogue. In both cases I advocate while illustrating the merits of blending theory and cultural studies with literary criticism in our still postmodern moment.

Rather than a standard interview, Chapter 5 enacts an engaged conversation initiated by a mid-career academic literary critic of American literature and culture. While he does not identify with theory, he is open and curious about it. The chapter offers a panoramic dialogue, on one hand, of insiders talking about teaching and textbooks; scholarly methods and writing styles; cultural studies approaches versus formalist close reading; the corporatization of the university; plus many facets of theory. Beyond academe, on the other hand, we discuss media, politics, and economics in the context of early twenty-first-century cultural conditions and the role of criticism today.

Chapter 6 opens up the question of the future of theory, a concern that recurs in subsequent chapters. In this initial case, it is the future of French theory. The chapter documents the unnoticed yet impressive array of ongoing posthumous publications of French theorists and the likely futures and revisions given the number of archives containing unpublished audio and visual as well as written sources, not to mention bootleg materials (some online). It illustrates the stakes of this question by examining the posthumous book publication of Jacques Derrida's last seminar. In this work Derrida puts on display for his audience not only his influential style of writing and his excessive mode of textual analysis, but his final reflections on smart reading and living on after death. In assessing Derrida's work, I show that deconstruction enacts, in an eccentric way, the work of critique in its combined ideological, cultural, and intimate registers. Derrida's distinctive mode of close reading, linked to the productive concept of a textual unconscious, will, I wager, continue to provoke theorists and antitheorists alike as the remaining 40-plus posthumous volumes of his seminars roll off the presses in coming years.

Chapter 7 extends the inquiry into the current second wave of French theory, its futures and its revisions, by addressing not the continuing avalanche of writing on it, but the surprising phenomenon of big biographies of French theorists like Barthes, Bourdieu, Deleuze, Derrida, Foucault, Lacan, and Levinas. The chapter gives pride of place to Benoît Peeters's *Derrida* (2010; trans. 2012), a biography steeped in the unpublished mammoth Derrida archives. Of particular note is this work's dispassionate documenting of innumerable telling real-life events including secrets. We readers get copious details on Derrida's politics, vexed lifelong relations with French educational institutions, and complicated relationships with peers especially Althusser, Bourdieu, and Foucault. We learn about Derrida's parents and siblings, wife and three sons (one illegitimate), and decade-long extramarital affair with philosopher Sylviane Agacinski, to whom he apparently wrote 1,000 letters. If this restrained biography had a thesis, it would be that Derrida, an outsider, lived life in excess. It's worth highlighting that the lives of celebrity academic intellectuals today merit biographies, autobiographies, and memoirs. People including scholars want to know about the real lives, no longer considered as private, behind the learned works. When asked in the documentary film *Derrida* (2002) what he himself would most like to know about past thinkers, Derrida said their sex lives.

If the turn of criticism and theory to life writing is surprising, the recent return of postmodernism as a period concept is altogether unexpected. So much had been written on postmodernism particularly during the 1990s that critics had tired of it by decade's end. Chapter 8 documents and supports the return, which started sometime around 2010. It reviews and refines seven examples, citing among others Ihab Hassan, Linda Hutcheon, and Christopher Jencks, pioneer theorists of postmodernism, all returning recently to the topic. In this chapter I argue for retaining yet rehistoricizing the postmodern concept.

Chapter 9 fleshes out the account of the twenty-first-century theory renaissance by focusing on half a dozen exemplary major books (personal favorites), discussing their strengths and weaknesses. While these texts address a wide range of pressing topics and illustrate a variety of current approaches, they share a focus on neoliberal political economy, identity politics, and today's corporate university. The chapter concludes with summary cameos on the renaissances of literary, critical, and cultural theory, plus a portrait of theory's relation, both productive and vexing, to today's corporate university.

In the form of an investment advisory letter, Chapter 10 sketches productive futures awaiting theory, highlighting its many strengths and contributions. It distinguishes between Theory Incorporated and the Theory Market, that is, between institutionalized theory courses, programs, and textbooks, on one hand, and theory fashions, hot topics, and jobs, on the other hand. It situates theory inside the corporate university, portraying the problems and promises of that location for the future of literary and cultural criticism.

* * *

Initial versions of several of my chapters appeared earlier in journals: Chapter 1 in *Minnesota Review*, Chapter 4 translated into Chinese in *Wai Guo Wen Xue Yan Jiu (Foreign Literature Studies)*, Chapter 5 in *Symplokē*, Chapter 6 in *Genre*, Chapter 7 in *SubStance*, and Chapter 10 in *Works and Days*. I am grateful for permission to revise and reprint. For professional interest and support, I thank colleagues Ronald Schleifer, Eve Bannet, Daniel Morris, and Zhu Gang, plus my research assistant Nancy El Gendy. I remain especially grateful to colleague and close friend Jeffrey Williams, who read and commented on the chapters.

1

What I believe and why

Although I completed my US PhD in literary studies during the 1970s, I didn't assert an explicit point of view, an identifiable critical position, until the 1980s. In an article I published in 1987, "Taboo and Critique: Literary Criticism and Ethics," I outlined my own project of cultural critique, fusing poststructuralism with post-Marxist cultural studies. First, I criticized the taboo on extrinsic criticism promulgated by the American New Critics and tacitly conveyed to me by most of my professors. Second, I sketched my own program by working through faults with the 1980s critical projects of Wayne Booth (liberal pluralism), Robert Scholes (structuralism), and J. Hillis Miller (conservative deconstruction), all major critical voices of the time. Where the New Critics focused on the literary text as an autonomous aesthetic object and explicitly forbade critics from linking it with society, history, psychology, economics, politics, or ethics, cultural critics of all stripes, myself included, accepted and affirmed such links. This is no easy road to travel. When Booth, Scholes, and Miller, furthermore, all insisted that close reading precede ethical critique, they retained a mandatory formalistic phase for critical inquiry, keeping the literary text as a privileged aesthetic object on the way to broadened social concerns. They got things backwards.

The 1987 article became the opening pages of my book, an unabashed credo, *Cultural Criticism, Literary Theory, Poststructuralism* (1992), arguing a handful of positions on perennial literary topics consistent with a fin-de-siècle US cultural studies informed by poststructuralism. It was evident in my piece that I had bought into cultural studies, having been earlier identified with poststructuralism, particularly Yale deconstruction. However, my first book, *Deconstructive Criticism* (1983), followed an arc from French structuralism and poststructuralism through Yale deconstruction to the *Boundary 2* group (cast as an alternative deconstructive project) to the wide-ranging anarchist projects of Michel Foucault and of Gilles Deleuze and Félix Guattari. In the end, it parodied Yale deconstruction. Things became even clearer with my next book, *American Literary Criticism from the 1930s to the 1980s* (1988). It covered thirteen schools and movements, starting with Marxism and New Criticism, adding as firsts for histories of American criticism four separate chapters on engagé social criticism stemming from the New York Intellectuals, Feminism, Black Aesthetics, and Cultural Studies. The work traced over the course of 500 sober pages both formalist projects that dehistoricize, depoliticize, and aestheticize literary studies and antiformalist movements that deepen and extend cultural criticism. My trajectory was clear.

In 1987, I got divorced after 17 years of marriage. Also, I moved from working at a small private Southern liberal arts university for 13 years to a large Midwestern state research university. When the dust settled, I ended up a single parent with two young teenagers. Over the next ten years, I shepherded them through high school and university. These were rough times. Up close and personal I learned about the economics and politics of postmodern culture.

On the verge of bankruptcy, having doled out $30,000 for legal expenses surrounding the divorce, I managed after 18 months of hand-to-mouth apartment dwelling to buy a house. It was done through creative financing by a Realtor along with his banker and appraiser colleagues. It appeared a miracle of free-market neoliberal economics. Why? I rented the house for six months. That became the 5% down payment. I obtained a subprime adjustable rate mortgage from a local bank, plus a small personal loan on the side from the Realtor. It all seemed a wonder, going from near-bankrupt to homeowner in 18 months. Lucky for me, the interest rate did not shoot up, nor did the price of houses drop. Eventually, I was able to refinance with a new fixed-rate mortgage, which, however, cost several thousand dollars in closing fees added to the principal of the loan. Debt proliferates.

As you might imagine, during this period I felt chronically insecure. I was fearfully checking interest rates on a regular basis. I witnessed to my astonishment the moral relativism ("flexibility") of the real estate, appraisal, and banking industries. By the late

1990s President Clinton solidified the changes going on, radically deregulating banking and investment, and tearing down key firewalls erected during the Great Depression by President Roosevelt. Branch banks started to pop up all over the place. Credit was increasingly easy to get. Home ownership rates were rising. And single-headed households were more and more common. Critics continue to confirm, initially in the wake of feminism, that the personal is linked with the social, political, and economic. My personal story felt more and more like an introduction to the politics and economics of our late postmodern era.

The day the Clinton White House announced a freeing up of student loans in the early 1990s, I was overjoyed and relieved as, it turned out, were bankers, politicians, and university administrators. My oldest child was just starting university on her way to BA and MA degrees—and ultimately $46,000 in loans, despite her scholarships, summer jobs, and Teaching Assistantship. My youngest child soon racked up on his BA degree $10,000 in loans. I don't recall anyone in my 60s generation carrying much debt for their college education, whereas my children, like the majority in the US, face a decade or two or three of debt repayments. (When I was a visiting Fulbright professor in Northern Europe in the 1970s, I witnessed free university education where students received additional support from state stipends.) So I was misguided to be overjoyed at President Clinton's apparent munificence, not realizing from the outset it was a way to shift financing from state institutions to individuals, enabling the government to withdraw from paying for education. I did not recognize nor condemn this move to privatization, but I did register it immediately in growing anxiety about interest rates, credit scores, debt loads, and the financial future of my children. There is a politics of feelings and everyday family intimacies that reveals to us what's really going on in the culture. This is intimate critique, an essential survival skill for our times.

At the same moment my children moved in with me, the continent-wide retirement system for many North American university teachers began to change after decades of stability. When during the 1970s I first entered TIAA–CREF (Teachers Insurance Annuity Association–College Retirement Equities Fund), there were two accounts where I could allocate my money (a sum equal to 10% of my annual salary contributed by my university): (1) TIAA Traditional [Bonds and Mortgages] (founded 1918) and

(2) CREF Stock (established 1952). Most new faculty members at that time split their funds 50/50% or 40/60%, with other permutations possible. Arriving at a new university position in 1987, I continued the split I had had at the previous job (this time the school contributed a figure equal to roughly 15% of my salary). But starting in 1988, things at TIAA–CREF began to change more and more tellingly over the next several decades. In 1988, a new choice was added to the earlier two—the CREF Money Market Account. In 1990, two additional investment accounts appeared, CREF Bond Market and CREF Social Choice. Over the course of the 1990s other far more risky CREF options became available: Global Equities (1992), Equity Index and Growth (both 1994), Real Estate (1995), and Inflation-Linked Bond (1997). Then in 2002, TIAA–CREF opened 18 separate mutual fund accounts to retirement contributions. The year 2004 witnessed seven brand-new Lifecycle Funds, complemented by three more such accounts in 2007. In 2006, nine other TIAA–CREF retirement-class mutual funds emerged. If you're counting, this means that instead of the two previous choices, I and several million other participants now faced four dozen choices within the TIAA–CREF family of funds. By 2014, the number had risen to 77 funds. During this period, many of us, especially me, got befuddled.

Along the way I wondered, do I or my colleagues know enough about stocks, bonds, real estate, indexes, rating agencies, and so on to make good investment choices? During the 1990s, like it or not, we were all being turned into individual investors. That for me was a worrisome new burden. Previously I did not read investment account prospectuses and quarterly reports, nor did I monitor investment news. When my home computer got linked to the Internet in the late 1990s, I began to monitor finances, as well as to work, on a 24/7 basis. If it were not for their rules limiting the number of trades each quarter, TIAA–CREF might have turned me into a day trader over the course of the 1990s. This is my personal experience with mainstream casino capitalism, the triumphalist neoliberal free-market dogma spreading from the 1970s, which went into hyper drive in the nineties. It has become harder and harder for me not to talk about the recent reconfiguration of money, mortgages, work, education, retirement, debt, and their impact on the family as well as day-to-day life. The way I see it, this is a mode of criticism we need. It is different from the impersonal speculative way many critics do critique. Nearer home, the industry calls it "financial literacy." I prefer the broader intimate critique.

The social as well as economic transformations of our times have affected me in dramatic ways. It first started to register on me and my family in the late 1980s and early 1990s. Before my generation, there were two divorces in my huge Irish-Italian American Catholic family, a social network rooted in Islip and Babylon Townships on the south shore of Long Island. In my generation, there have been several dozen divorces, plus lots of mobility given a nationwide job market. Personally, I feel I have been living in exile as migrant labor since I got my first job in the South, followed by positions in the Midwest and the Southwest—four decades away from "home" and counting. The single-headed household, often uprooted from the extended family, caught up in mortgage and student debt, increasingly worried about health care expenses plus retirement, and befuddled by financial choices, describes not only my reality but that of so many others in the dramatically shrinking middle class. I hasten to add that my two siblings, an older sister and a younger brother, have long shuttled in and out of the working poor, a new and growing class of the nickled and dimed, without retirement accounts, health insurance, or owned homes. So much for the world of family values.

The psychological syndrome that fits our late postmodern social insecurity is, I believe, panic attacks. I've had them. This is different from the paranoia typical of the Cold War period of my youth. Panic attacks involve more or less continuous stress, anxiety, and distraction, compounded by overwork, caffeine, sugar, excessive options at every turn, speed, multitasking, a 24/7 reality, too much news and media, an absence of quiet time and relaxation, not to mention leisure. Some people seem to thrive on this regimen. The rising generation appears more adapted to it, texting like bandits while popping anxiety pills in record numbers.

The mode of criticism that is best suited to these times, it has seemed obvious to me, is a renewed ideological and cultural critique with political economy, particularly finance, at center stage. It also has to deal with the feelings, emotions, and intimacies that social tides set in motion. Increasingly since the 1980s, I have felt that my job as a university professor entails teaching not only protocols of close reading but techniques of cultural critique.

Unplanned happenings, unexpected events, and accidents have played a decisive role in my personal life and career. Very early on, my economics teacher at the state Merchant Marine academy in New York told me to consult Heilbronner's *The Worldly Philosophers* for my course project on nineteenth-century economic theory. When I asked a librarian about worldly philosophy and Heil-something, he sent me to Heidegger. A fateful event. I was 18 years old and just opening to the world of literature, philosophy, and economics, but with neither direction nor mentor. Two years later, following a Do-It-Yourself immersion in existentialism, Beat literature, and left Keynesian economics, I walked out of this military academy liberated (no more uniforms) and became a literature major.

The month after I started on my new road, my younger brother, a high school senior, died in a drunk-driving car accident. That had the effect of solidifying my anger at God into agnosticism and bouts of atheism. My eleven years of rigorous Cold War American Catholic education, all in uniform, predating the liberalizations of the Vatican II Council and teaching dreadful medieval dogmas, prepared me poorly for the world. Not surprisingly, I am a long-time secularist, who believes in freedom from religion as well as freedom of religion. I have little good to say about fundamentalisms, which have visited members of my family as well as a broad swath of the globe. I am nonplused, if bemused, by New Age spirituality. I retain respect for liberation theologies. But, in general, I keep a wary eye on religion.

I had to play catch-up on literary studies, being two years behind my cohort. So I undertook a three-semester MA to compensate and satisfy my curiosities. The week I graduated a military draft notice arrived. It was a few days before Christmas, and I was applying for PhD programs. Quickly I took a six-month spring semester teaching job in a local high school to earn money and to forestall the draft. It was 1968, and I decided unequivocally I would go into exile to Canada or possibly Sweden if I were drafted into the Army. Vietnam changed forever my feelings about American imperialism and nationalism, teaching me the necessity of critical patriotism. The Vietnam War was stupid, immoral, and criminal, as was the post-9/11 war in Iraq. Later in this book, I shall have more to say about family, education, religion, government, and other spheres of socialization and ideology.

Let me jump ahead. By chance I was asked to referee a proposal in autumn 1994 for a "Norton Anthology of Literary Theory and Criticism." The publisher turned to me, I figured, because of my prior books. I ended up endorsing the idea of a Norton anthology devoted to theory, but not the specific proposal, recommending against the proposer, sketching what shape a proper anthology should take, and listing who should be considered for the job (not me). A few months later the editor showed up in my office and asked me if I would be interested. I hesitated but ultimately accepted with two understandings: that I could recruit a team of editors, and that revised editions, if deemed desirable, would happen on roughly eight-year rotations. I didn't want the anthology to become a way of life and a full-time job. And I believed a collective approach to the task, never tried before with large theory anthologies, made the best sense. This was summer 1995. Luckily, it was an opportune moment for me because I had just finished the manuscript of my book, *Postmodernism—Local Effects, Global Flows* (1996). As it turned out, my next book was the *Norton Anthology of Theory and Criticism* (2001), with me as general editor along with a team of five handpicked editors. The opening page of the Preface, drafted by me and approved by the team, defined "theory" this way for new generations of students and faculty:

Today the term encompasses significant works not only of poetics, theory of criticism, and aesthetics as of old, but also of rhetoric, media and discourse theory, semiotics, race and ethnicity theory, gender theory, and visual and popular culture theory. But theory in its newer sense means still more than this broadly expanded body of topics and texts. It entails a mode of questioning and analysis that goes beyond the earlier New Critical research into the "literariness" of literature. Because of the effects of poststructuralism, cultural studies, and the new social movements, especially the women's and civil rights movements, theory now entails skepticism toward systems, institutions, norms; a readiness to take critical stands and engage in resistance; an interest in blind spots, contradictions, distortions (often discovered to be ineradicable); and a habit of linking local and personal practices to the larger economic, political, historical, and ethical forces of culture.

This is what I believe. And I came by it the hard way. It is not my teachers's theory. It's a survival skill for our times that I advocate throughout this book.

My motivation for undertaking the anthology project was largely missionary. After I completed my PhD on the history of poetry and poetics, I converted to criticism and theory as a specialty. There were no such specialty programs when I was coming up. Like others in my cohort, I "reengineered" myself over the next decade through self-directed study, research, and teaching interrupted with short periods of formal postdoctoral education: Summer Seminar funded by the National Endowment for the Humanities (1976), School of Criticism and Theory (1978), Fulbright-Hays Theory Lectureship (1979), International Institute for Semiotic and Structural Studies (1981), Alliance Française in Paris (1982). I also completed a bachelor's program in French while I was working as a beginning professor during the 1970s. In its post-formalist first wave, theory in North America was vital, exciting, life-enhancing, not the narrow and deadening dogma of the previous era. I was a convert.

For me the *Norton Anthology of Theory and Criticism* (2nd ed., 2010) was, and is, designed to accomplish several missions: to dignify and monumentalize theory; to consolidate the many gains of contemporary theory; to defend theory during the culture wars, which were started by the antitheory right-wing in the mid-1980s and persist today; most important, to introduce students and faculty, in the US and abroad (where nearly half of its sales happen), to a wide-ranging, provocative, and accessible textbook that is both scholarly and up-to-date, being constructed from the standpoint of twenty-first-century cultural critique. (Forgive the promo.) I see myself as both an insider and a populizer. I make no apologies to my hierophantic colleagues. The mission lives on.

Here is a piece of illuminating background. I was flabbergasted and bitterly angry when I heard ex-CIA agent Philip Agee on a 1970s late-night television interview explain how in the 1950s and 60s the CIA recruited candidates at Catholic colleges. Why Catholic colleges? It turns out the CIA preferred to recruit there because Catholics understand hierarchy, discipline, and duty. "Son of a bitch," I spluttered. From kindergarten to tenth grade (ages 5 to 16 years), I was enrolled in Catholic schools. I wore a uniform every day and marched to class, went to confession on Saturdays, attended 9.00 a.m. mass in uniform each Sunday. They taught me acquiescence to authority, selflessness, and endless rules (preconditions for fascism). As a theorist, I teach skepticism toward authority, self-assertive cultural criticism, and intimate critique.

My *Postmodernism—Local Effects, Global Flows* was followed by *Theory Matters* (2003) and *Living with Theory* (2008). All three books practice cultural criticism rooted in theory. What holds this later work together is an ongoing project of mapping as well as evaluating postmodern culture. I construe postmodernity as neither a philosophy nor a movement nor a style, but a new period that started in the 1970s and has continued to morph until this day. I have more to say about it in Chapter 8. Not uncritically, I am working in the wake of Fredric Jameson, David Harvey, and the British New Times project (Hall and Jacques), all dating from the early 1990s and continuing into the new century. My experience and observations confirm that we are still living in a postmodern culture, a distinct post-Welfare State period, more or less helpfully labeled postindustrial, post-Fordist, consumer society, late capitalism, and globalization.

What most dramatically characterizes postmodern culture for me is disorganization. Think of the TIAA–CREF case. On the one hand, financial consumers are offered an excessive array of choices of investment products pitched to their tolerances for risk, time frames, and preferences. On the other hand, who has the time and expertise to make intelligent choices? I'm confused, stressed, perplexed. I seek a guide for idiots or dummies, the latest edition since the pace of change is rapid. This is a symptomatic genre for our times. As a wine drinker (my Italian heritage), I am befuddled by the number of decent Chardonnay and Syrah/Shiraz wines under $20 a bottle. This largesse dates from the wine revolution starting in the 1970s. *Wine Spectator* magazine (established 1976) nowadays evaluates 20,000 wines annually. I have a similar experience in a bookstore (for example, the self-help section), a supermarket (the cereal aisle), a footwear store (walls of sneakers). The speeded-up proliferation of commodities and choices, plus the disaggregation of niches and spheres, render the big picture perhaps knowable yet unmasterable. Hence, the value of mapping. Theory has not escaped postmodern disorganization, a claim I graph in Figure 1 and discuss in this book.

One last unexpected turn of events helps explain what I believe and why. I couldn't find a position the year I received my PhD, the

US literature job market having crashed several years earlier (1970 to be exact and continuing today). So, I ended up teaching on a one-year interim appointment in the Department of Humanities at the University of Florida. There I met Gregory Ulmer, a new PhD in Comparative Literature who had just secured a full-time tenure-track job. Two decisive things occurred during that year. First, Ulmer introduced me to French theory. That shook me up and helped me get past my New Critical training and frame of mind. Second, the job required me to teach multiple sections of Humanities 211, 221, 231 during the fall, winter, and spring quarters. The course content was set by the department, with only a few open spots. One step ahead of the students, I learned and taught Ancient & Medieval, Renaissance & Enlightenment, and Modern Western Humanities. The curriculum programmatically juxtaposed art history, literature, philosophy, religion, and music (with the latter handled by a musicologist in large lectures). A typical module would be the Parthenon, Plato's *Republic*, Sophocles' *Antigone*, and Aristotle's *Poetics* or Abstract Expressionism, Existentialism, Beat Literature, and Bebop Jazz. Although it covered old-fashioned intellectual rather than social history, the program put me in touch with big pictures. It struck a resonant cord within me. Early and late, my work has instinctively aimed for wide-ranging comparative history.

The program also introduced me to art history (specifically architecture, sculpture, and painting). Out of this material came a life-long interest in contemporary painting, plus modern museums, galleries, art journals and books, and local art scenes. When I first came to think about postmodernism, I naturally turned to painting as well as to literature, philosophy, and popular arts (I am a child of the 60s). One of the genuine benefits of construing postmodernism as a period, not just a school of philosophy or a style, is the necessity to investigate political economy and society as well as the arts high and low. Postmodern fusion, multiculturalism, and backlash manifest themselves, I find, in the period's food, wine, fashion, film, music, art, philosophy, religion, literature, and theory. Through accidents and blindly, it appears, I was being prepared and preparing myself early on for a job of cultural criticism and critique. Our times demand it.

2
Antitheory

There are a dozen or more identifiable contemporary antitheory factions in North America and the United Kingdom. It's an odd phalanx. Among them are traditional literary critics; aesthetes; critical formalists; political conservatives; ethnic separatists; some literary stylisticians, philologists, and hermeneuticists; certain neopragmatists; champions of low and middlebrow literature; creative writers; defenders of common sense and plain style; plus some committed leftists. What most characterize many of the antitheory factions as well as independent and maverick critics of theory are arguments calling for a return to the close reading of canonical literature, for clear writing of critical prose that avoids obscurity and jargon, and for settling disagreements through reasoned argumentation rather than statements of personal beliefs. Antitheorists often complain bitterly about contemporary theory's commitments both to social constructionism (versus scientific truth and objectivity) and to multiculturalism with its critical focus on race-class-gender analyses. For their part, theorists refer to antitheorists as the "I love literature crowd." I'll unpack this loaded accusation as I progress through this chapter. When tolerated at all by antitheorists, theory serves as a handmaiden to appreciation of literary texts. In no case should theory become autonomous, a separate field, or a new academic discipline. This is a consecration to be accorded only to literature itself.

With its 48 pieces written over three decades, *Theory's Empire: An Anthology of Dissent*, edited by Daphne Patai and Will H. Corral and published in 2005, remains the bible of contemporary antitheory arguments. It is a hodgepodge, with selections from such notables as René Wellek, M. H. Abrams, Marjorie Perloff, Tzvetan Todorov, and Denis Donoghue. They are brought together to criticize theory, defend the canon of great works and literary analysis, uphold a commonsense realist theory of language, and excoriate the politicization of literary study characteristic of much contemporary theory. The general point of view is conservative, characteristically looking backward to earlier better times and approaches (the modern versus the postmodern). As the title suggests, the thesis of this doorstop volume is polemical: theory during the postmodern era has come to dominate literary studies, creating in the process an enduring empire and an orthodoxy. So, the critics of theory are here marshaled as anti-imperialist dissenters against empire. It is a telling self-aggrandizing conceit.

In this chapter, I portray a half dozen of the best of the best antitheorists and their arguments, offering my own assessments. Then I return to the big picture and the two editors' summary of claims against theory. My primary argument is that we should not have to choose between theory and antitheory. My secondary argument, foregrounded from start to finish here and also in Chapter 3, is that an account of contemporary theory is incomplete without accounting for its many adversaries. The phenomenon of antitheory constitutes a revealing segment of the history of theory. To file it away under "culture wars" or the "battle of the ancients versus the moderns revisited," while provocative, is shortsighted. Much can be learned from the antitheory phenomenon about contemporary literary studies, the corporate university, and cultural politics.

Taken from his book *Literature Lost: Social Agendas and the Corruption of the Humanities* (1997), John Ellis's "Is Theory to Blame?" gathers the theory of the closing three decades of the twentieth century under the banner "race-gender-class theory." Ellis has been among the most visible and active of the antitheorists starting in the 1980s. His explicit standpoint is postwar Euro-American formalist stylistics as embodied in the landmark book, *Theory of Literature* (1949), coauthored by René Wellek and Austin Warren. As a historian of theory, nothing attracts his favorable attention after the 1950s. On key issues of theory, such as the nature of authorial intention, literary quality, and historical context, mid-century theorists are purportedly far more complex, convincing, well-informed, committed to analysis, independent, and original than their thankless present-day heirs. For Ellis, contemporary race-gender-class theory is simple-minded, ill-informed, dogmatic, and conformist. Furthermore, the topics of real concern today, long debated in the history of criticism, receive unsophisticated handling. Nowadays, nothing is new, just diluted. Standards of argumentation and logic have deteriorated. John Ellis's mission is to save *real* theory from *bad* theory: "what now passes for theory is a degraded and corrupt shadow of what theory should be" (106). What has been especially disturbing, historically speaking, is the becoming fashionable of theory and its jargon: "As theory became fashionable, there arose a theory cult in literary studies, and its leadership became a kind of theory jet set, a professional elite with a carefully cultivated aura of au courant sophistication. In this atmosphere, only recent theory counted; anything from earlier times was wooden and out-moded. The persistent ignorance of prior theory was therefore no accident but an essential feature of this new development" (104–105).[1]

Obviously lumping all post-1950s theory under the category race-gender-class is a problem. While it might apply in a way, however unflattering and homogenizing, to ethnopoetics, feminism, New Historicism, queer theory, Marxism, postcolonial theory, or cultural studies, it does not depict psychoanalysis, hermeneutics, structuralism, deconstruction, reader-response theory, or poststructuralism. Theory is not one thing.[2] So, the charge of "political correctness," proffered by Ellis, amounts to a dismissive as well as careless slur. Also, Ellis's definition of real theory and theorists is narrow and prescriptive. Real "theorists do not run in packs; they are individuals who set out to crack particular

---

[1]John Ellis emerged as a leading figure in the culture wars that started during the 1980s and continue today in the US. Early on, he occupied the roles of defender of traditional Western humanities and critic of theory. In 1993, he cofounded the Association of Literary Scholars, Critics, and Writers, an affiliate of the National Association of Scholars (founded 1987), both conservative organizations with antiliberal agendas. The ALSCW had and has as a main goal to create an alternative organization to the Modern Language Association (founded 1883). Many antitheorists are hostile to the 30,000-member MLA for accommodating theory. In its initial years between 1994 and 2007, ALSCW received more than thirty grants from well-known right-wing foundations, primarily Bradley, Olin, and Scaife, reaching a million dollars (www.mediatransparency.org). ALSCW and NAS have Websites with archives.

[2]For six different current definitions of theory, see my "Theory Ends," *Living with Theory*, chap. 1.

problems by thinking hard about them. Their work is solitary; it is never fashionable and must always be estranged from orthodoxies…. Real theorists thrive on the concept of argument and counterargument that is central to theoretical analysis, but race-gender-class scholars show a marked tendency to avoid facing the substance of the arguments of their critics" (105–106). This view proposes a Great Man and solitary genius theory of cultural history that not only dissolves historical context but also discounts forerunners. Ironically, it does not apply at all to Ellis's beloved formalists, who ran in packs and became fashionable members of a reigning orthodoxy. Ellis damns everything that comes after the 1950s, a time when he was a student. He positions himself as a resentful defender of the old guard, a curmudgeon.

Insofar as advocates of new paradigms often ignore earlier competing paradigms, Ellis is misguided to expect the formalist tradition to be carefully examined as opposed to rudely dismissed by postformalists. For example, Yale-educated theorists Harold Bloom, Stanley Fish, and Stephen Greenblatt were trained by leading formalists but turned away from them with very little looking back or reasoned argumentation. They are prodigal sons (J. Williams). Intellectual change is often abrupt; it need not be respectfully conformist. Ellis is a poor historiographer. Moreover, his antitheory attacks leave out of account larger social dynamics such as the contemporary corporatization of the university and its requirements for productivity and innovation, not to mention its related nurturing of an elite star system. It makes little sense to form judgments on the role of contemporary theory in the absence of the historical transformation, for good and ill, of the university. Not surprisingly, the advent of multiculturalism, liberal diversity management, and their theoreticians uniformly constitute disasters in Ellis's unnuanced account.

One of the most lucid and earliest contemporary antitheory arguments appears in M. H. Abrams's short piece "The Deconstructive Angel." This memorable paper was originally delivered in the 1970s at a session of the annual convention of the Modern Language Association. On the panel were Abrams (distinguished literary historian), Wayne Booth (advocate of Chicago school critical pluralism), and J. Hillis Miller (leading deconstructive critic). What prompted the panel was an earlier hostile review by Miller of Abrams's book *Natural Supernaturalism*. Miller cast the book as an example of "the grand tradition of modern humanistic scholarship" (6), whereupon he proceeded to critique the tradition in the name of Derridean and de Manian deconstruction. Wayne Booth wanted the antagonists to debate their differences publicly. Abrams portrays himself on the panel as a traditional historian of Western culture and a critical pluralist, meaning someone tolerant of different approaches to linguistic and historical interpretation. In his presentation he offers, first, fair-minded and cogent accounts of both Derrida's and Miller's theories of language and interpretation. Second, he cleverly counterpoises his own ideas.

Just before Miller is to make his presentation, the last of the three papers, Abrams concludes his argument with a telling witty prognostication about Miller's talk:

> I shall hazard a prediction as to what Miller will do then. He will have determinate things to say and will masterfully exploit the resources of language to express these things clearly and forcibly, addressing himself to us in the confidence that we, to the degree that we have mastered the constitutive norms of this kind of discourse, will approximate what he means.... What he says will manifest, by immediate inference, a thinking subject or ego and a distinctive and continuant ethos.... (209)

Each feature of discourse singled out in this mock praise of Miller constitutes a component of Abrams's commonsensical pragmatic account of language posited over against deconstruction's counterintuitive theory of discourse. For Abrams, speakers and writers use norms and conventions of language, including professional language, to express more or less determinable thoughts and feelings. They can be masterful or not, clear or not, and we the audience will make sense of these utterances crafted by individual persons. These persons possess consciousness, distinctive identities, and certain intentions. They are capable not only of initiating discourse but also of mutual understanding.

Deconstructive accounts of language for their part highlight the potential indeterminacy of language, most notably in polysemous literary and philosophical texts. *Finnegans Wake* comes to mind. Connotations always precede the orderly denotations of the belated dictionary makers. Grammar compounded by rhetoric (tropes are ineradicable) introduces slippage and uncertainty in language. Innumerable bits of previous intertexts run through texts (historical assemblages) beyond any accounting. Moreover, authorial intentions are not so much inferred as assigned always in retrospect with certain interests and prejudices, conscious and unconscious, in reserve. Here is how Abrams, exaggerating more than slightly, characterizes the upshot of Miller's deconstructive theory: "what it comes to is that no text, in part or whole, can mean anything in particular, and that we can never say just what anyone means by anything he writes" (206). Such deconstructive critical skepticism weakens the grounds for objective literary and historical interpretation, Abrams's main concern to support and defend.

What bearing does this debate have on the antitheory phenomenon? Early on and up to the present moment—for four decades—"theory" has often too simply meant deconstruction, that is, Derrida and his followers first at Yale University and then elsewhere. The common phrases "after theory" and "posttheory," echoed in so many titles of books and articles starting in the 1990s, signify both "after the triumph of deconstruction in the 1980s" and "after its supercession during the 1990s" by the growing successes of postcolonial and ethnic theory, the spread of new historicisms, and the emergence of queer theory and cultural studies. Occasionally, "posttheory" and "after theory" get broadened and designate what comes after "French theory." But actually what comes after is more theory and often influenced by deconstruction. The ubiquity and dissemination of deconstruction's notorious critiques of "binaries" testify to the survival of this particular theory. I have in mind the many critical inquiries up to today scrutinizing traditional hierarchical binary conceptual pairs, for example, nature/culture, masculine/feminine, human/animal, self/other, conscious/unconscious, and normal/abnormal. These pairs recur in major Western literary and philosophical discourses and are topics of contemporary concern. My point is that there is no after theory—or after deconstruction—pure and simple. What there is is a devout wish for theory's demise, meaning the eradication of deconstruction and poststructuralism, plus their legacies. For the editors of *Theory's Empire*, Abrams's paper furthers that cause and is all to the good.

In his "The Rise and Fall of 'Practical' Criticism: From I. A. Richards to Barthes and Derrida," taken from his book *Double Agent: The Critic and Society* (1992), Morris Dickstein, a fourth-generation New York intellectual, argues from the standpoint of a self-willed amateur non-specialist independent literary critic (yet distinguished professor). He addresses a shrinking educated public and champions clear style and commonsense. Not surprisingly, Dickstein is unhappy about the professionalization of literary criticism, criticizing its jargon, its impotence and willed separation from the public sphere, and its deadening irresponsible formalisms. In addition, he deplores recent critics' careerism, intellectual cleverness and narcissism, plus pedagogy's dumbing down of literary criticism. Morris Dickstein identifies with the great canonical literary figures. For him genuine literature is meaningful, vital, and experiential, despite its fictional forms and artificial conventions. While critical analysis must attend to formal technical features of art, its most important focus must be on affective and philosophical matters, that is, truly human concerns: "The test of a critic comes not in his ideas about art, and certainly not in his ideas about criticism, but in the depth and intimacy of his encounter with the work itself—not the work in isolation, but the work in its abundance of reference, richness of texture, complexity and feeling" (64). The theory that Dickstein explicitly faults is formalism, whether the brilliant technical analysis pioneered by I. A. Richards in the 1920s or the admittedly clever poststructuralist decodings of Roland Bathes and Jacques Derrida in the late twentieth century.

Theory has an important secondary meaning in Dickstein's argument, namely presuppositions, particularly any ones that disable openness to the new. That is to say, Morris Dickstein positions himself as an independent modernist critic reliant on his educated sensibility. He lets us know in passing that he spent time at Yale and Cambridge Universities. He has no business with critical methods and movements. He presents himself as the last of the independents. He positions himself back in the fin de siècle with Henry James and D. H. Lawrence before the advent of Anglo-American formalism, before the thorough academic professionalization of literary criticism, before the fall. He exhibits mixed feelings about the tradition of modern periodical criticism. On the one hand, this mode of learned journalism addresses the public in a lucid manner, yet on the other hand, it is partisan, uncivil, and identified with one group or another. It is no surprise that Morris Dickstein's review of twentieth-century theory fails to mention psychoanalysis, feminism, ethnopoetics, or postcolonial theory. These are telling omissions from an isolated connoisseur. What we have here is an articulate and moving yet backward-looking conservative liberalism unhappy with postmodern conditions as well as high modernist trends. The best one can say is that Dickstein sensitively registers the brilliance of Richards's and Barthes's theorizing while discounting technical analysis and, by omission, cultural critique in favor of literary appreciation informed by history and individual sensibility. Dickstein's strong antitheory position is sui generis.

Eugene Goodheart's "Casualties of the Culture Wars" (2005) is clear and straightforward in its defense of aesthetic criticism against ideology critique.[3] His ultimate goal is to make peace between these two warring camps of the culture wars. He presents himself as an elder statesman. The main job of literary criticism for Goodheart is the interpretation and evaluation of literary works in the context of history. He is a critical pluralist tolerant of other approaches and perspectives. The task of aesthetic criticism entails appreciation and discrimination not only of craft and content but of personal experiences and emotions. The critic has a trained sensibility. Amateurs are out. Scholarship is the sine qua non of proper criticism. The distinctive features of literary aesthetics for Goodheart consist of several kinds (although he doesn't package them this way): (a) rightness and splendor of language, wit and ingenuity; (b) imagination and beauty, pleasure and power especially familiar from the sublime in art; and (c) disinterest, freeplay, and ineffability. What distinguishes his treatment of aesthetics is an openness to impurities and entanglements. He is wary of the mystifications coming from advocates of pure aesthetics and art for art's sake. While politics and morality admittedly play roles in aesthetics from Shaftesbury, Addison, and Hogarth to Kant, Schiller, and Arnold, Goodheart holds out for distinctive aesthetic experience. In this, he joins contemporaneous parallel turns to affect theory, to new formalisms, and to a return to literature.

What most typifies American criticism and theory since the 1970s is, according to Goodheart, a shift from formalism to ideology critique. It's a stark Manichean vision he offers. "Ideology critique rules the roost" (510), he declares ruefully. Thus the editors of *Theory's Empire* cast him as an antitheorist. Ideology critique

---

[3] Eugene Goodheart's article in *Theory's Empire* melds extracts from two earlier works by him: *Does Literary Studies Have a Future* and "Criticism in the Age of Discourse."

suspects behind everything the operations of interests. Its faults are many for Goodheart. It construes the task of criticism as the uncovering of hidden interests. This hermeneutics of suspicion is morally righteous and reductive. It refuses debate (argumentation, evidence, logic). It abjures and anathematizes aesthetics. It practices bad prose style without any concern for elegance or clarity. It has no interest in literary sensibility and taste other than to be suspicious of them. It disregards open-mindedness and objectivity, letting beliefs take the place of knowledge. Finally, "there is nothing more aggressive than the effort to demystify the supposed illusions of others" (510). Who are these practitioners of ideology critique, according to Goodheart? It's a loose, not to say violent, assemblage of theory-affiliated schools and movements: Marxism, structuralism, feminism, poststructuralism, deconstruction, New Historicism, postcolonial theory, and cultural studies. Goodheart paints with an impossibly broad brush creating caricatures.

Eugene Goodheart positions himself as a liberal centrist against the extremisms of left and right cultural camps. One problem is he doesn't detail the problems of the right. Another is he doesn't define ideology other than as interests (hidden, disguised, or open). There is a great deal more to this venerable concept, for example, the base/superstructure dialectical model of society. To get a sense of Goodheart's ultimately vehement antitheory stance, consider the progression in this statement: "Ideology critique can be a valuable activity if it knows its limits, discriminating between what requires and what does not require demystification. In contemporary practice in the academy, it has become an imperial obsession with disastrous consequences" (510–511). Here emerges the metaphor of theory as imperialist empire. There are a handful of revealing passages where Goodheart, the Manichean, tries to strike a balance between left and right, ideology and aesthetics, critique and criticism (his oppositions). "The critic need not, indeed cannot, avoid talking about ethical, political, religious, or historical issues. What is decisive is the way he speaks or writes about the work, the kind of attention he gives to what counts as aesthetic qualities. An aesthetic response foregrounds the work and doesn't allow it to be devalued by one or another discourse" (513). This is Goodheart's modest proposal. He is motivated to make it because he foresees no going back to earlier times of aesthetic criticism free from ideology critique. As with many other antitheorists, the tone here is a mixture of sadness and outrage. Still, Goodheart seeks balance and a middle way. The love of literature always comes first. That's the main point, plus of course the criticism of theory. These are doubtlessly the two main reasons the editors include him in *Theory's Empire*.

Among the sharpest critics of theory from the middle generation is Mark Bauerlein, high- profile cultural warrior, English professor, and defender of the humanities. In his article, "Social Constructionism: Philosophy for the Academic Workplace," published by *Partisan Review* in 2001, he notes unhappily that social constructionism has become the dominant epistemology of the contemporary humanities, especially literary theory. He defines social constructionism succinctly: "It is a simple belief system, founded upon the basic proposition that knowledge is never true per se, but true relative to a culture, a situation, a language, an ideology, or some other social condition" (341). Key terms of contemporary theory that embody this noxious standpoint include antifoundationalism, contingency, and situationism, plus the slogan of many theorists following Fredric Jameson's famous axiom "always historicize." Pitted against such relativisms are truth, objectivity, knowledge, and facts, all subject to verification, validity, and argumentation, none of which concepts and procedures social constructionism bothers with.[4] The latter is a belief system, not an epistemology. Touchstones for Bauerlein are science and logic. In ignoring and refusing debate (logic, evidence, justification), social constructionism shows itself to be a dogma, a creed, replete with a party line and an attitude. Representative theorists (constructionists) singled out by Bauerlein include Michel Foucault, Richard Rorty, Terry Eagleton, Stanley Fish, Eve Sedgwick, and Paul Lauter. These social constructionists are committed to a morality of social justice not a real epistemology open to philosophical scrutiny. They do not label their concepts as opinions, hypotheses, or speculations. They should. In argument, they operate through psychology not epistemology, proceeding ad hominem. It is no use, therefore, to point out that social constructionism commits the genetic fallacy or is a form of relativism.

---

[4]Compare Amanda Anderson, who examines the nature of argumentation amongst theorists, especially feminists, poststructuralists, and pragmatists, from a Kantian Habermassian perspective that promotes critical reflection. In 2008, Anderson became Director of the School of Criticism and Theory, the venerable summer institute that has trained 2,000 theorists since 1976.

Why has social constructionism, asks Bauerlein, been so successful in the humanities? He offers a persuasive hypothesis:

What has emerged from social constructionism is not a philosophical school or a political position, but an institutional product, specifically, an outpouring of research publications, conference talks, and classroom presentations by subscribers. For many who have entered the humanities as teachers and researchers, social constructionism has been a liberating and serviceable implement of work, a standpoint that has enhanced the productivity of professors. (348)

Bauerlein explains further that the US academic tenure system today requires a beginning professor in the humanities to produce a book manuscript within three and a half years of hiring. This speedup means long-term projects and careful methods no longer serve. He rues the day that humanities professors let the quick book become the main criteria for tenure ("lifetime security"). As a result, beginning "professors will avoid empirical methods, aware that it takes too much time to verify propositions about culture, to corroborate facts with multiple sources, to consult primary documents, and to compile evidence adequate to inductive conclusions" (350). Facts, objectivity, and truth fall by the wayside. In short, social constructionism has been successful because "it is the epistemology of scholarship in haste, of professors under the gun. As soon as the humanities embraced a productivity model of merit, empiricism and erudition became institutional dead ends, and constructionism emerged as the method of the fittest" (353).

Bauerlein positions himself here as both critical of the current period and nostalgic for slower, more deliberative yet unspecified earlier times. He appears in the role of conservative defender of traditional humanities and transcendental truths based on reasoned method. It's a "timeless" ideal yet borne of modernity. He is hostile to all manner of contemporary theory and postmodernity as his list of social constructionists suggests (against poststructuralism, neopragmatism, post-Marxism, reader-response theory, gender and queer theory, plus cultural studies). Nonetheless, he is a penetrating critic (unaffiliated) of the contemporary corporate research-oriented university—with its addiction to productivity, speedup, and short-term accountability. He presents his Darwinian theory—a mode of historical and ideological critique after all—that social constructionism is a fit response to savage productivity demands as a hypothesis, a hunch. Scientific method requires such a gesture of modesty.

But Bauerlein has forgotten that the great leap forward in research and publication productivity was spawned by early Cold War-era formalism, especially New Criticism. Its successful formula for book writing survives to this day: a first chapter on a critical approach or method followed by four or five chapters of close readings of individual texts. Productivity does not stem from social constructionism. It derives from the business management model undergirding the research university established in the 1950s and 1960s and culminating with the corporate university of recent decades.

The corporatization of the university associated with the dominant economic paradigm of laissez-faire late capitalism is not Bauerlein's target, although it should be. Productivity demands come from where? Like most antitheorists in *Theory's Empire*, Bauerlein is no social critic, nor does he want to be. Yet social currents run through his as well as their arguments in very obvious yet repressed ways. For Mark Bauerlein, the standard of truth is Newton's law—true in all times and all places. Such knowledge is not relativistic social construct. The humanities today, rightly defensive and in a survival mode, need to emulate scientific truth. That is Bauerlein's main point, which ironically happens to be an antihumanistic belief, one could argue. In any case, he finesses the tension between science and culture.

Given the dominance of cultural studies in recent decades, the wide-ranging critique by Stephen Adam Schwartz, titled "Everyman as Übermensch: The Future of Cultural Studies," is both relevant and au courant. It's a good place to conclude this critical survey of antitheory sentiments and arguments. Published originally in 2000 in *SubStance*, a North American journal of contemporary French literary culture, Schwartz's essay targets cultural studies as theorized and practiced especially in US English departments. He is a professor of French language and literature, an interested but dispassionate outsider. What is wrong with cultural studies? Most of the piece is given to impersonal exposition and critique of its various features and faults. Many faults are listed. Nothing good is said. Cultural studies is antidisciplinary and antimethodology. Hélas. It promotes popular culture and explodes the literary canon, jettisoning aesthetic value and distinction. It remains suspicious of social institutions in their support of norms and their policing of deviances. It buys into social constructionism, regarding knowledge as always enmeshed with both interest and power. It reduces facts to mere values and points of view. There is no neutral epistemological space in its faulty perspective. Cultural studies sees all of reality as a social construct, including notably science, literature, and truth. It is committed to a project of demystification, not appreciation. It buys into cultural relativism. It is unremittingly hostile to all hierarchies. Most importantly, it has a flawed concept of culture entangled with idiosyncratic notions about politics.

The idea of culture propounded by contemporary culture studies, argues Schwartz, pits master narratives against particular ones. It is always a matter of hegemonic and counter-hegemonic forces in struggle, where cultural studies sides predictably with subaltern, subcultural, and multicultural minorities. It routinely celebrates resistance, transgression, and difference. In this sense it is reminiscent for Schwartz of modernist avant-gardes, especially surrealism: both end up with ineffectual content-poor politics and merely aesthetic vanguardist appeal. What most characterizes the culture concept of cultural studies, claims Schwartz, is its surprising foundation in "the *individual* and his or her preferences." "In other words, individuals—replete with a full set of interests, desires, and beliefs—come first and culture is something not only derived and secondary but pernicious and, therefore, ultimately unnecessary. Personal preferences—*someone's* choices—turn out to be lying behind all collectively shared categories" (373). This charge of individualism leads Schwartz to project for cultural studies its unspoken utopia. He portrays an antihierarchical and leveling cultural studies depicted as an incoherent polyphony, an indistinction, of equally valid voices. Cultural studies "ends up with an epistemological and political anarchism rooted in the purest individualist voluntarism" (376). In a final twist of his argument, Schwartz concludes that cultural studies, after all, promotes the modern Western ideas of egalitarianism and expressive individualism, being just one more seemingly radical form of individualism in our time.

It takes guesswork to know what Stephen Adam Schwartz's own standpoint might be. He keeps it tightly under wraps. His highly dramatized description of cultural studies is fair enough, except for the characterization of its ideas on culture and anarchism. Pace Schwartz, cultural studies exhibits a distinctively leftist anarchism, not a disguised rightwing libertarianism: it privileges the community over the individual. That is the upshot of race-class-gender analyses. In addition, there is no way that culture is unnecessary or secondary in cultural studies theory. It is inescapable. It molds individuals ineradicably. We are born into culture, its norms, conventions, and prejudices. It is more or less clear that Schwartz wants to respect hierarchies and preserve canonical literature over against popular culture. He is a critic of social constructionism and apparently a believer in classical canons of objectivity, truth, and disinterestedness. All that is evidently more than enough to make him a dissenter from the contemporary empire of theory and a card-carrying antitheorist.

From the point of view of the long history of criticism and theory ranging from Gorgias and Plato to bell hooks and Judith Butler, it's a mistake to equate theory with contemporary cultural studies, or French theory, or any one school or method. The panorama especially in our time is much wider than all that. It's a rich age of theory, varied and complex. A main fault of antitheorists is a blindness to this bigger picture and to the renaissance of theory and criticism during recent times. This blindness accounts for why the antitheory campaigns undertaken during contemporary culture wars sometimes evoke from theorists comparisons with earlier struggles between ancients and moderns. The polemical point is that moderns always win, incorporating yet transforming, sometimes drastically, ancient traditions.

The editors of *Theory's Empire*, Professors Patai and Corral, add a final document to their antitheory anthology (a moral coda to their story). It's a two-page excerpt from Wayne Booth's book, *Critical Understanding: The Powers and Limits of Pluralism* (1979), titled "A Hippocratic Oath for the Pluralist." It propounds five basic rules to insure critical justice as well as to reduce the onslaught of published criticism and theory. The five admonitions to critics are: read before you write about a text; understand before critiquing a text; remain suspicious of texts and critiques; take the time necessary for a project; and be self-critical. Here is Booth's closing homily addressed to fellow academic literary critics:

> Using these five simple ordinances, we could quickly reconstruct our experience of criticism: we would write and read only about one-fourth as many critical words; we would experience

a renewed sense that our critical sanity does not depend on "covering" as many works as possible; and we would find leisure to enter full-heartedly into those that met or expanded our interest and heightened pleasure and profit from what we did read. (689)

The gist is that the reconstruction of criticism and theory depends on more time to read and write fewer critical works, a lot fewer, 75% less. The problem is we are drowning in published scholarship and its main consequences, namely, fast reading, quick writing, and superficial coverage. Missing from the current regime are leisure time, expanded interests, and real pleasure and profit in reading criticism. Clearly, Wayne Booth's oath harkens back to another simpler time, wishing for a different higher education system and a better society, as so much antitheory does. Yet the editors gloss the oath this way: "The spread of Theory has made this call more necessary now than when it was written" (687). Whatever else one can say about this poorly targeted commentary, it blames theory for sins it did not commit, and it is very obviously not a model of Booth's patient pluralism or of his well-known pro-theory sentiments, just the opposite.

My own arguments against contemporary theory, if I can generalize, come down to a half dozen or so complaints. Too many theorists' writing style lacks clarity and economy, not to mention elegance. A related problem is a relative lack of attention to formal craft, stylistics, and aesthetics, not that I want criticism done by strict formalist checklists. Some theorists are righteous and pious to the point of stern intolerance, where tone veers off badly. I have no problem with pleasure reading, a life-enhancing mode of "nonacademic" criticism that many theorists discount or overlook. I understand but worry about the utilitarian tendency among academic theorists to reduce all theories to formulaic approaches and methods as quickly as possible. Then there is the problem of market vanguardism, that is, theorists jumping on the latest theoretical bandwagon no matter what it might be. Some theorists are more interested in being provocative than convincing; it should not be a choice between these two values. Last but not least, too many theorists to this day downplay the shaping context of the corporate university, with its demands for productivity, its onslaught of publications, its 55-hour work week, its addiction to cheap adjunct labor, its proliferation of student debt, and its obsession with research innovation and grants. But all things considered, these complaints do not add up to a case against theory.

The vehement antitheory line of the editors of *Theory's Empire* is pounded into readers' heads across the 15 pages of the Introduction. It lacks the nuance of many of its contributors and of Wayne Booth's pluralist oath. Nothing good is said about theory. The indictment is long on theory's sins and faults. The editors' self-declared point of view is resolutely 1950s formalist criticism, stylistics, and aesthetics focused upon literature (not culture). That's *the* alternative to "theory." The definition of literature is taken for granted. All formalist analyses are homogenized retrospectively into one newly desirable mode of criticism. No differences are highlighted or suggested, for example, among the many individual formalists and formalist groups (for instance, Moscow, Leningrad, and Prague schools; American New Critics and Chicago Critics; Kenneth Burke vs Cleanth Brooks vs Murray Krieger).[5] No faults of formalism are recorded, nor are the many disputes among stylisticians, aestheticians, and formalists examined. None of the innumerable critiques of formalisms receive attention. The editors' allegiance to formalism is thin, uninformed, and defensive.

The closing argument of the Introduction fabricates, not to say socially constructs, a common sentiment—an incredible credo—for the 48 antitheorist contributors: "All share an affection for literature, a delight in the pleasure it brings, a respect for its ability to give memorable expression to the vast variety of human experience, and a keen sense that we must not fail in our duty to convey it unimpaired to future generations" (14). While I can't think of a single theorist who would disagree with this sentiment, disagreement would surely erupt over the concept "human experience." Does it, for instance, include experiences related to race, class, gender, nationality, and subject formation? Evidently not, or only if these are subordinate to literary pleasures. Taboos come quietly into place here. Criticism's job is to serve literature and to read "literature as literature" (6). So much for human experience. This is an unsupported, dogmatic version of the old American formalist heresy of paraphrase. It casts

---

[5]See my *American Literary Criticism Since the 1930s*, especially Chapters 2, 3, and 9, which differentiate in detail more than a half dozen modes of formalism.

"theory" (reduced to ideology critique) as "textual harassment" and political allegory (8). But in light of the numerous schools, movements, and subdisciplines of theory during recent decades, "Theory," this bogeyman of the editors, capitalized here, is a stark instance of othering, scapegoating, and politicizing. It is a grandiose homogenized allegorical figure: the Big Bad "T."

The editors have a strong political orientation that goes undisclosed. None of the vast body of antitheory works produced on the left gets excerpted or even mentioned in *Theory's Empire*. Fredric Jameson's early critique of structuralism is missing, so is Edward Said's attack on deconstruction, plus Mary Louise Pratt's on reader-response theory, all three well-known and dating from the 1970s.[6] Innumerable other sources, early and late, could be cited, including many published during recent times.[7] But only right-wing and centrist antitheorists appear in *Theory's Empire*. The editors' attempt at depoliticizing literary studies, like so many other antitheorists's similar attempts, fails abjectly.

I believe literary criticism, in its practice and its theory, in publications and classrooms, should employ technical analysis of craft, aesthetic appreciation, and both ideology and culture critique. The latter includes intimate critique rooted in personal experience. Such methods and approaches are not mutually exclusive nor should they be. Projects of antitheory to purify or reconstruct the discipline of literary studies risk resuscitating formalist taboos against "extrinsic" concerns (namely, politics, economics, history, sociology, psychology, morality, theology, biography, and reader response). Much of human experience and of the world is thus cordoned off or rendered peripheral. Criticism gets ferociously emptied and rarefied. This is a way to insure the further mummification and antiquation of literature in our time. If it came down to it, I would probably choose, speaking hypothetically and tactically, a middle-way liberal centrist project of keeping literary works at the core of criticism with extrinsic matters at its periphery over the arch conservative enterprise of magnifying the literary work and outlawing its

---

[6]My *American Literary Criticism Since the 1930s* surveys the critiques as well as the tenets of leading theorists and schools.

[7]For wide-ranging leftist critiques of contemporary theory, see, for varied instances, Timothy Brennan and Michael Bérubé.

worldly "contexts." But why should I have to choose? And should my students be subject to such a mandatory truncation of critical perspectives? The *via negativa* of much formalist and aestheticist antitheory enacts a drastic renunciation, a displaced religious zeal, against the world. It's a theologizing of literature and its acolyte criticism. Count me out. However, count me in on the critique of productivity speedups characteristic of contemporary free-market society and corporatized education. I support the old goal of a 30-hour work week. But antitheorists refuse to talk about such matters. My point is it's shortsighted and foolish as well as authoritarian to restrict the worldly topics fit for discussion amongst literary critics.

I am aware that formalist aesthetics during the interwar period, especially the 1930s, constituted a tactic for safeguarding the arts and literature from fascist and state communist censors, book burners, and executioners. It provided protection, sought freedom, and devoutly wished for autonomy. Yet art for art's sake carries a politics that very much alters depending on context and circumstances. Given certain conditions, it can become dogmatic, antihumanistic, and reactionary, as it frequently risks doing amongst contemporary antitheorists.

I have a coda to add and a confession to make in closing this chapter. In their Introduction to *Theory's Empire*, the editors indict half a dozen recent theory anthologies. They include the *Norton Anthology of Theory and Criticism*, on which I serve as general editor along with five associate editors. So I stand indicted. The two editors charge the leading anthologies with various shortcomings such as grandiose ambitions, promoting theory about theory in place of love of literature, advocating ideology critique, and omitting leading antitheorists.

I hasten to add that the *Norton Anthology of Theory and Criticism* does not come in for special treatment in *Theory's Empire*. It is presented as one of many such anthologies. It represents a trend. That being the case, I don't know whether to be relieved at escaping personal buffeting or to be irritated because the distinctive features of the Norton project go unmarked. Yet there is something much bigger at issue that the editors deplore. They nickname it big "T" Theory.

The antitheorist editors of *Theory's Empire* have no problem with theory (little "t") where it means approaches to literature and its appreciation, or textual methods and tools, or rational reflection and argumentation. But when theory is narrowly equated with or limited to structuralism, deconstruction, and poststructuralism—French theory—they complain and rightly so. There is so much more to theory, starting especially with many more contending contemporary schools, approaches, and subfields mostly ignored by the editors. The real problem for them is big "T" Theory.

Let me provide some background to contextualize this issue otherwise. Many new fields of inquiry were born in the late twentieth century, the early years of the postmodern period. Some have developed into new breakaway disciplines housed in separate academic departments; others have been situated in interdisciplinary programs (rather than fully funded departments); and still others have become subdisciplines of traditional disciplines. Examples of new humanities departments, programs, and subdisciplines—location and status depending on each institution—include African American Studies, American Studies, Creative Writing, Film and Media, Linguistics, Semiotics, Rhetoric and Composition, and Women's Studies. In the sciences there are similar instances such as Biochemistry, Computer Science, Immunology, and Nanotechnology. In the social sciences, one finds new areas like Cognitive Studies, Econometrics, and Gender Studies. Where does theory fit in this epochal transformation and how does it get defined?

On the one hand, theory in recent times has become a crossover interdiscipline fusing literary criticism, linguistics, philosophy, history, anthropology, sociology, psychoanalysis, and politics. It possesses a distinctive postmodern identity captured in contemporary theory anthologies. On the other hand, it remains a subdiscipline housed in traditional departments such as English and comparative literature. There are no autonomous departments and only a few semiautonomous programs of theory in the Anglophone world. In other words, theory remains subject to literature in most jurisdictions while maintaining a sense of independence, especially from the traditional service functions of criticism, specifically narrow textual explication and exclusive aesthetic evaluation. Meanwhile, the modes of critical reading have multiplied and the value of canonical literature has been relativized under pressure from excluded minorities and from popular culture and media. So, it is in the name of pre-postmodern discipline and the old order that antitheorists call theory to its role as handmaiden to literature (defined adamantly as canonical belles lettres). Anathema, therefore, is theory (big "T") as speculation, multiculturalism, populist cultural studies, ideology critique, antihumanism, intellectual vanguardism, academic celebrity culture or, worst of all, an interdiscipline engaged in explicit transdisciplinary projects. This is big "T" Theory swollen with grandiose ambitions. For the humble editors of *Theory's Empire*, it signals a lamentable degeneration. They deplore the self-enclosed jargon-ridden arcane world of Theory and call it back to the proper love of literature:

> We believe that in the thirty years between the publication of the first edition of Hazard Adams's *Critical Theory since Plato* [1971] and the appearance of the *Norton Anthology of Theory and Criticism* [2001], much has been lost with respect not only to theory and criticism that actually illuminate literary texts but also to the appreciation of criticism's actual contributions to academic discourse. That time span also saw the dissemination of theoretical principles in innumerable books aiming to ease readers' way into the arcane world of Theory, while in no way encouraging a love of literature. (6)

The message to Theory is clear: get back where you belong, the appreciation of literature. Put first things first. Reverse the tragic decline. Restore the canon. Fall in line. Declare your love for literature. I love literature. I say, I love literature.

I have responded to such arguments on several occasions in defense of theory, as, for example, in my manifesto *Living with Theory*.[8] So I won't rehearse those efforts here. The way I see it, the editors of *Theory's Empire* represent a conservative countercurrent—a politically oriented center-and-right front they summon to arms in retrospect—in order to defend formalist and aestheticist modes of literary criticism against innumerable heresies

---

[8]See also *Norton Anthology of Theory and Criticism*, 2nd edition, which contains celebrated antitheory essays as well as canonical and contemporary pieces advocating formalism and aesthetics. The Alternative Table of Contents lists nine selections under the category "Antitheory." They represent a very broad spectrum of critical perspectives (humanistic, scientific, aestheticist, formalist, and epistemological), coming from left, right, and center.

of criticism and theory.[9] They speak for a true faith in all its purity and issue condemnations in its name. While they can't admit it, many antitheorists are critical of contemporary postmodern society for its disorganization, proliferation of options, and miscegenations (fusions, pastiches, hybridities). Core traditions appear in tatters. A problem for antitheorists is that I, myself a Theorist (big "T"), love literature, and I doubtlessly represent most theorists in saying so. An even bigger problem for antitheorists is that we Theorists insist on examining how the I of "I love literature" works, and who gets to define "literature," and where and why certain critical oaths of allegiance and related condemnations come about both in the past and the present. Critical inquiry creates disruption. It can be accused of corrupting society especially students, as we know, which is the case with much accusatory antitheory. In the end, there are many ways to love literature. Attacking theory has not helped.

---

[9]The literary Web blog, the Valve, which was hosted by ALSCW, sponsored one of its Book Events—a roundtable book review, chat, and promotion—on *Theory's Empire*. The edited proceedings with contributions from two dozen academics and a brief Afterword by Patai and Corral is available from Parlor Press in free PDF format or in standard book form compiled by John Holbo. The Valve has been inactive since March 2012.

3

The tasks of critical reading

The modes and conventions of academic critical reading have proliferated during the contemporary period, prompting continuous fusions and flexibilizations. An early pioneering illustration of such eclecticism would be Marxist feminist deconstructive postcolonial cultural criticism—the kind of blended critical approach associated since the 1970s with Gayatri Chakravorty Spivak. At the same time, various antitheory backlashes have called for returns to the common reader, close reading, and appreciative aesthetic criticism. Such calls have gained renewed momentum in the twenty-first century. Most are shortsighted. Against them I want to define and to defend a minimum program for practicing and teaching critical reading today. This approach blends close reading, ideology critique, and cultural critique with intimate critique and pleasure reading. In this defense, I make no claims for originality, but rather for balance, range, and relevance.

I am motivated to make this statement by recent disturbing articles calling for uncritical, reparative, appreciative, surface, generous, and renewed close reading. None of these are my terms. What they share is both weariness with and growing aversion to ideology and cultural critique, plus a longing for something new and enlivening. Insofar as they promote pleasure reading and close reading, I am sympathetic. Where I have problems is in excluding or deemphasizing ideology and cultural critique, a vexing and untimely tendency especially during our neoliberal era and continuing Great Recession.

I begin this chapter with a consideration of pleasure reading and arguments against critique and then move on to close reading, ideology critique, and cultural critique. I discussed intimate critique in Chapter 1 and revisit it here. I conclude with summary remarks and defense of a broad-based critical reading.

Pleasure reading

In the case of pleasure reading, two celebrated ethnographic studies—specifically of readers of romance novels by Janice Radway and of tight-knit communities of television fans by Henry Jenkins—illustrate complex systems of interpretive conventions, critical standpoints, and institutional matrices undergirding leisure-based reading (Leitch 2008). Despite opinions about it, pleasure reading is neither simple, nor disengaged, nor uncritical, quite the opposite.

Nevertheless, critics especially academics often consign pleasure reading to the sphere of appreciation, of subjective reading, of uncritical response (Jacobs). In this whole way of categorizing, a revealing system of polar opposites and a structure of feeling operate.

Poles of Reading
critical/uncritical
scholarly/popular
objective/subjective
suspicious/trusting
professional/amateur
depth/surface
slow/fast
heavy/light
laborious/pleasurable
rigorous/impressionistic
disinterested/interested
edifying/entertaining
sophisticated/crude
learned/naïve

According to traditional learned opinion, pleasure reading is uncritical, light, naïve, impressionistic, and subjective. It is characteristically fast moving, crude, entertaining, and amateurish. Conversely, serious reading is critical, sophisticated, rigorous, objective, slow, suspicious, and deep. It is associated with work rather than leisure and with edification not entertainment. Academic taboos have long neatly cordoned off light and uncritical pleasure reading from learned and careful critical reading. Never the twain shall meet.

This standard account contains stereotypes, straw men, and loaded words like "naïve" and "light." The values engendering this entire concatenation of oppositions derive ostensibly from Enlightenment-era classical philology, official scriptural hermeneutics, and especially modern literary criticism as solidified during the rise of the university and the professions. But contemporary postmodern ethnographies of reading have effectively disrupted these long-standing oppositions (Towheed, Crane, Halsey). Let me illustrate with an example, Radway's *Reading the Romance.*

Janice Radway studies 42 lower-middle-class women readers of romance novels living in a Midwestern American suburb (Radway). They are connected through a bookstore and a newsletter. Radway's ethnography of this reading group subverts the standard bifurcation of reading into critical versus uncritical. She details the protocols of these readers: they read rapidly, often skip to the end, pay no heed to style, ignore critical distance, identify with characters (especially heroines), and care most for plot. They are given to elaborate interpretations of the motivations of male protagonists. They share prescriptive criteria: no violent heroes, no weak heroines, no pornography, no unhappy or uncertain endings. They are voracious readers who occasionally reread favorite works particularly when depressed. For these heterosexual readers, the romance novel is compensatory, illustrating ideal relationships over against the status quo of distracted partners in a world of too much or no employment. While this is a local interpretive community of fans, of appreciative fast readers of popular literature, they are also attentive, steeped in the tradition of contemporary romance and armed with elaborate generic as well as emotional and social criteria. These are hardly uncritical readers focused only on appreciation and surface details.

The spread of academic cultural studies has for decades dignified popular culture and its fandoms, recognizing the sophistication of heterogeneous interpretive communities (Machor and Goldstein). But when it comes to romance and other genres of "pulp literature," academics themselves still too frequently remain predisposed to superficial and subjective, unsophisticated and interested, that is, uncritical accounts. So let us continue to promote pleasure reading yet without scorn.

Against critique

Unhappiness with academic critical reading, notably critique, exists today among a growing number of critics. It has prompted an array of articles promoting alternatives. Pioneering the way, Susan Sontag famously declares herself against interpretation in favor of immediate sensuous and non-utilitarian response (Sontag). Her imagined model is primordial ritual activity and magical experience preceding the burdens of consciousness. In the process, any and all critique gets tossed out the window. This is phenomenology in a pure form. For her part, Eve Kosofsky Sedgwick, late in her career, recommends reparative reading over against so-called paranoid reading (Sedgwick). Updating Paul Ricoeur's famous observation, she complains that much contemporary reading partakes of the hermeneutics of suspicion, specifically Marxist criticism, psychoanalysis, Nietzschean-style genealogy, feminism, and New Historicism. She sets the hope, pleasure, and contingency of reparative reading, as found in phenomenology, aesthetics, and New Critical formalism, against the purported anxious cynicism, pain avoidance, and demystifying determinism of the above-named "hegemonic" paranoid modes of academic reading. Here pleasure reading, appreciation, and close reading explicitly supplant ideological and cultural critique. Critical enchantment trumps disenchantment. Relief is at hand.

In our new century a growing chorus of critics, like Sedgwick, bemoan critique and propound alternatives. Mark Edmundson calls for a moratorium on "readings" by which he means the application to a literary text of a specialized vocabulary such as Marx's, Freud's, or Foucault's (Edmundson). He wants students and critics to encounter directly and sensitively the author's view of life, of how to live, of what to do. Interpretation and criticism come afterwards. Appreciative existential openness to the text is a laudable goal. But a bogus sequencing and prioritizing is folded here into a wish for old time simplicity. In the process of reading, criticism and interpretation don't simply wait upon personal response nor should they.

Yet another alternative is Rita Felski's neophenomenology. Felski finds problems with the critical detachment, dispassion, and suspicion that she claims characterize the contemporary discipline of academic literary criticism. She foregrounds personal enchantments, which distinguish ordinary as well as academic reading, and that respond to the fundamental question of why a text matters. "Critique needs to be supplemented by generosity, pessimism by hope, negative aesthetics by a sustained reckoning with the communicative, expressive, and world-disclosing aspects of art" (33). This declaration stages a dramatic yet untenable either/ or where a both/and choice makes more sense. The mechanical parade of polar oppositions here is startling and unconvincing. Still, Felski's muted call for balance heads in the right direction retaining critique.[1]

For his part Michael Warner sympathizes with "uncritical reading," depicting academic critical reading as specialized and antiquated. "Critical reading is the pious labor of a historically unusual sort of person" (36). It purportedly privileges distance, disengagement, and repudiation while putting a premium on the individuality of the modern enlightened reader. Moreover, notes Warner, it presupposes learning, privacy, and note taking, plus the paged codex as opposed to the continuous scroll of today's Internet. Warner's uncritical readers (especially undergraduate students in his literature classes) employ nonacademic protocols. They identify with characters, worship authors, seek information, skim, laugh, and cry. In this context, critical reading of any sort appears rarefied, old-fashioned, very near its end. The problem is that Warner does not credit or examine the protocols of close reading and critique employed by student readers. He assumes they are naïve and out of touch with critical skepticism and naysaying. As I see it, he slips into stereotypes in pitting uncritical against critical reading. In harshly

---

[1] Compare Catherine Belsey who condemns current academic critique as pious and dogmatic, calling for a return to aesthetic pleasure and textual analysis. Belsey's sui generis project rests upon a peculiar Lacanian theory of pleasure in which literature (like language) stands in for the unattainable "lost object" (primordial nonlinguistic Real life). What motivates Belsey is an explicit vanguardist search for the new and shocking. This explains why she can depict today's academic feminist and postcolonial cultural critique as "conformist" and "orthodox" preaching to the converted (27).

For a self-conscious, middle-of-the-road balancing of close reading and ideology critique, see the project of Weinstein and Looby, who acknowledge at the outset of their collection of eighteen essays by diverse hands "the inextricable entanglement of aesthetic and ideological matters and the necessary critical virtue of keeping their dynamic interrelationship in constant play" (7).

portraying professional critical reading as an ideology, a subculture, and a self-interested ascetic discipline—a direct rival to uncritical reading—Warner ironically exploits the very tools and techniques of critical reading that he bemoans.

The modes of uncritical reading profiled here are characteristically much too thinly conceived in light of ethnographic studies analyzing conventions and practices of pleasure reading. They offer caricatures and lack balance, turning away from critique.[2] Students appear infantilized.

Close reading

Recent calls for "close reading" ring hollow in my ears. Why? To begin with, there are numerous very different modes of such reading. In the absence of specifics, the mantra to "return to close reading" seems to me both unexamined and insincere. If you wonder what modes of close reading I'm referring to, I respond briefly with a list of six variegated well-known examples: Cleanth Brooks's formalism in *The Well Wrought Urn* (for instance, his first chapter on John Donne's "Canonization"); Martin Heidegger's ontological phenomenology in "Language" (an essay on Georg Trakl's poem "Winter Evening"); Erich Auerbach's philology in "Odysseus' Scar," the opening chapter of *Mimesis* contrasting Homer and the Old Testament; Roman Jakobson and Claude Lévi-Strauss's famous structuralist demonstration article "Charles Baudelaire's 'Les Chats'"; Jacques Derrida's deconstruction in "Plato's Pharmacy"; and Roland Barthes's poststructuralist semiotics in *S/Z* (an exhaustive book analyzing Balzac's story "Sarrasine"). But rather than multiplying further different modes of rigorous close reading, which would be easy enough (Caws; Lentricchia and DuBois), I want to checklist the

---

[2]Compare Bruno Latour, who rightly worries about the opportunistic uses of critique by antievolutionists, deniers of climate change, and debunkers of science. However, he does not renounce critique. See also Jacques Rancière's criticism of left- and right-wing critique, both of which treat the general populace as incapable imbeciles. In mounting his own critique, Rancière defends his long-standing axiom of the equality of anyone with everyone.

main protocols and premises of Cleanth Brooks's formalist style of close reading—long a setter of norms for North American academic critical reading.[3] The contrast with Radway's readers of romance is instructive.

Here are ten key rules of formalist close reading in the New Critical manner of Cleanth Brooks.

1 Select a single short canonical literary text, preferably a lyric poem.

2 Avoid personal emotional response in favor of objectivity.

3 Rule out historical inquiry in preference to stylistic and aesthetic analysis.

4 Carry out multiple retrospective readings.

5 Presuppose the text is intricate and complex, efficient and unified.

6 Subordinate incongruities and conflicts in the interest of overall unity.

7 Show paradox, irony, and ambiguity resolving disunities.

8 Treat the text as impersonal drama and well-made autonomous aesthetic artifact.

9 Focus on patterns of imagery, metaphorical language, and literariness and not, absolutely not, on psychology, morality, sociology, or political economy.

10 Try to be *the* ideal reader.

Given these criteria, we can see why most New Critics might consider John Donne a better poet than Walt Whitman. But I don't want to rehash in depth the relative strengths and weaknesses of this early Cold War highly influential aestheticist

---

[3]Franco Moretti's advocacy in *Graphs, Maps, Trees* and elsewhere of "distant reading" (in explicit opposition to close reading) is a call for the statistical analysis of data concerning sales figures of novelistic subgenres over long historical eras. While I have a few quibbles with this valuable mode of quantitative historical criticism, I am critical when it unnecessarily dismisses both close reading and critique in pursuit of illuminating yet reductive graphs and maps. Moretti is director of the Stanford Literary Lab, a center specializing in quantitative literary analysis. See its online series of pamphlets for examples of distant reading.

reading formation. Nor do I wish to trash Brooks. What interests me in this manual of procedures and these evaluative criteria are stark differences from the critical charter shared by Radway's romance readers. A reader of romance could subscribe to none of these critical premises, and a New Critical formalist could abide none of the ten protocols earlier specified for romance readers. I could go on here to compare and contrast the many modes of close reading mentioned above, their differences, overlaps, and preferences. Yet I won't. My aim is not only to call into question the standard system of values associated with the distinction between critical and uncritical reading, but also to suggest the baggage as well as insincerity of vague calls for a return to close reading. There is more to be said about such baggage.

Many contemporary pitches for close reading, first launched in the culture wars of the 1980s and 1990s and ramped up in the new century, appear to me to be efforts either to restore the canon of great literary texts, or to undo the "triumph" of theory, or to call us academics away from cultural studies and critique, or all three (see, for example, Patai and Corral discussed in Chapter 2). Moreover, some calls are antiacademic, some anti-intellectual, and others willful vanguardist provocations. Behind old and new campaigns for close reading lie an array of wishes and curses. A few samples will clarify my point. There is the wish to restore the common reader (Teres; Gioia; NEA), which I see as an alluring but mythical figure.[4] There is a desire to return to earlier aesthetic analysis and evaluation accompanied frequently by curses on contemporary identity politics, ideology critique, and popular culture gone viral (Ellis). There is widespread unhappiness about and resistance to the

---

[4] For Harvey Teres, the common reader is a nonacademic who derives aesthetic pleasure from appreciating the craft and beauty in any art form high or low (2). But here commonality and reading are hollowed-out metaphorical concepts. For his part, Dana Gioia offers a perplexing elitist portrait of common readers (his term), a very uncommon well-to-do group, 2% of the population, "our cultural intelligentsia" (*Can Poetry Matter?*, xviii and 16). In its 2009 report on literary reading, the National Endowment for the Arts treats common reading improbably as a neutral technique used by 113 million American adults. While aggregating massive data, it pays no attention to standpoint, interests, interpretive protocols, aims, or critique. Common literary reading is rendered an insubstantial statistical chimera.

ongoing deaestheticizing transformation of literature into a media commodity stripped of its aura and entangled with commercial circuits of entertainment production, distribution, and consumption. There is ambivalent dismay at the growing demand for research productivity within the corporate university; it is this requirement of publish or perish that allegedly lies behind the success of theory, cultural studies, and critique, accounting for the proliferation of contending interpretive communities (Bauerlein). Let me reiterate, the catchphrase "close reading" carries a great deal of baggage. To make sense of it requires consideration of context and motives, which are, not surprisingly, value laden, debatable, and frequently opaque.[5] None of my commentary is to deny the value of close reading, which I strongly advocate and practice in my own teaching and research.

Ideology critique

The concept of ideology in most contemporary versions operates, as is well-known, on two premises of Marxist theory lately enhanced. Like formalist close reading, it has proven to be an extremely useful heuristic for critical reading and for classroom teaching. Let's not scrap it. Premise one, human history evolves unevenly through successive modes of production, spanning from tribal hordes, kinship societies, plus despotic and slaveholding societies to feudalism, capitalism, socialism, and communism. Class antagonisms, often repressed, mark each social formation. Starting around 1500 in the West, capitalism has gone through various stages, with postindustrial

---

[5]In her calls for restoring close reading to the center of literary studies in our time of new historicisms and cultural studies, Jane Gallop makes her motives and the context unusually clear. What renders literary studies a professional discipline distinguishable from history and sociology is close reading. To abandon it would be "disciplinary suicide" ("Historicization," 184). In addition, close reading furthers an "antiauthoritarian pedagogy" ("Historicization," 185) that empowers students. Gallop's definition of close reading, however, is thin. It consists of late twentieth-century US New Criticism and de Manian deconstruction unproblematically merged. It focuses both on language not ideas or paraphrases and on odd textual details not presuppositions ("Close Reading," 16). Clearly, Gallop's defensive call to close reading constitutes retrenchment in the face of real and growing threats to the humanities.

free-market neoliberal or late capitalism in the ascendency since the 1970s, going global in the 1990s, and intensifying during recent years in the face of severe economic crises. Premise two, the socioeconomic elements of society constitute its infrastructure while cultural spheres compose its superstructure, with both being linked and mediated through continuous horizontal feedback loops. The superstructure encompasses, significantly, family, religion, politics, law, education, unions, technoscience, and culture (Althusser). (This rundown of institutions from Althusser offers a useful checklist for students as well as cultural analysts.) Not incidentally, "culture" here designates crafts, sports, and the arts, high and low, literature included (R. Williams). Each of the superstructural spheres is more or less autonomous while being differentially connected to social totality. (Totalizing here entails linking your self to the social world and its institutions.) In this context, ideology consists of the ideas, beliefs, values, plus worldviews of the dominant groups in society that circulates through the superstructural institutions, including literature and popular culture. Ideology is what often passes for commonsense or doxa ("what everybody knows"). Undergraduate students, however, often mistake ideology as "personal" opinion. But it is just the opposite. This knee-jerk reversal in the interest of programmatic hyper individualism turns out to be a productive issue to pursue in the classroom. One can start a discussion with the claim that individualism is an ideology.

Ideology critique of contemporary film or historical literature, to take two instances, is capable of turning up a great deal about art, culture, and society. Why renounce it? It's a powerful and essential mode of critical reading. Consider a focus on the family, its definition and major forms, its relations with work and religion, its strengths and weaknesses. A teacher-critic of contemporary discourse can pose a handful of pressing questions with this heuristic in mind. According to cultural documents, how do things stand with, say, the North American family in the context of intensified postindustrial capitalism? Are there any changes of note? In what ways does the family relate to earlier forms and emerging ones? What enhances and what tears apart families now? Is there an ideal family? In recent domestic novels and television dramas, how is the relationship between individualism and family solidarity portrayed? In what ways are things depicted with the extended family and the nuclear family vis-à-vis traditional monogamy, serial monogamy, single-headed households, domestic partnerships, and living alone or in community? However depressing it might be to cast the family as an ideological unit, if you are a parent teaching your children the importance of hard work, self-reliance, and punctuality, you realize you are a spokesperson, a conduit, a carrier for innumerable impersonal norms and values that circulate throughout society and individuals, yourself included. Literature is such a conduit as is social discourse. This cannot and ought not to be denied. Should we scrap such insight in a project of purging ideology critique? Absolutely not.

During recent decades ideology critique has been enhanced with accompanying concepts, most notably hegemony/counterhegemony, commodification, utopia, plus the imaginary à la Louis Althusser, Fredric Jameson, and Slavoj Žižek. As with close reading, there are many different conceptions of ideology critique (Eagleton identifies more than a half dozen). The spread of these newer concepts coincides with the rise and triumph of free-market fundamentalism starting in the 1970s. "It is no accident." This familiar phrase summons the long-standing rule of thumb for ideology critique "as in the base, so in the superstructure." As capitalism goes increasingly global enabled by and enabling instantaneous financial and media flows, concepts of hegemony, commodification, a better world, and our imagined relations with reality become illuminating as well as inevitable. Consequently, I can't envisage teaching or practicing critical reading of literature, popular culture, or social discourse today without employing ideology critique, whether narrowly construed or enhanced. That would be malfeasance. The same goes for close reading in one form or another. These modes of reading are not mutually exclusive.

Cultural critique

I see cultural critique, speaking historically, as separable from ideology critique, although other critics and scholars do not (e.g., Ebert; Best and Marcus). There is a bit of confusion surrounding these terms. The postmodern race-class-gender analysis characteristic of cultural critique adds race and gender during the 1960s and thereafter to preexisting modern class analysis dating back to the interwar era, if not earlier. During the closing two decades of the twentieth century, cultural critique, associated with the new social movements of the 1960s, added to race and gender, which stemmed from the civil rights and women's movements, sexuality and nationality, deriving from LGBTQ movements and ongoing movements against (neo) colonialism. That said, in the Anglophone world many critics fuse modes of critical reading stemming from race and ethnicity studies, postcolonial studies, and queer theory with Marxist as well as psychoanalytic theory. They often call this postmodern blend cultural critique, sometimes ideology critique, or sometimes symptomatic reading.[6] Cultural critique is the predominant term today. It is distinguished by its flexibility and openness.

Among the most prominent of many modes of cultural critique is, to take one example, Foucaultian analysis. Michel Foucault depicts critique explicitly as calling into question reigning orders, norms, and institutions (so-called knowledge-power networks), especially of law, morality, and science (Foucault). He does this in the context of desubjugation and self-formation. Judith Butler crisply characterizes Foucaultian cultural critique as at once ethical, aesthetic, and political practice, putting it to good use in her early work of gender demystification (Butler). More recently, Michael Hardt self-consciously adds to Butler's Foucaultian-style critique an engagé focus on modes of political activism that he extrapolates from the later lectures of Foucault (Hardt). He advocates a militant Foucaultian critique "that has the power to struggle against the

---

[6]In most variants, the term "symptomatic reading" designates the fusion of ideology and cultural critique. See, for example, Stephen Best and Sharon Marcus's survey of the many positive examples and types of so-called "surface reading" all set over against the bogeyman "symptomatic reading," which they associate with Marxism (in a Jamesonian register), psychoanalysis, and contemporary cultural critique. Crystal Bartolovich pointedly criticizes this project of surface reading and defends Jameson-style Marxist ideology critique.

In a related article advocating nonjudgmental and generous "eventful" reading over against emotion-laden and identity-based "suspicious" reading, Timothy Bewes contrasts in passing Althusser's and Jameson's versions of symptomatic reading (8). He equates most theory with pontification and excoriates it while promoting a singular project of asceticized phenomenology rooted in renunciation of standpoint and self. The via negativa of this radical program of close reading—or unreading—magnifies the terms of the text while erasing the reading subject's words. It calls for the death of the reader. Like much twenty-first-century neophenomenology, this project exhibits no awareness of its greatest precursor, namely Geneva phenomenology. See also Armstrong's preliminary integration of the phenomenology of reading with contemporary neuroscience.

life we are given and to make a new life, against this world and for another. Beyond critique's ability to limit how much and in what way we are governed, this militancy opens up a new form of governance" (34).

Cultural critique, Foucaultian and otherwise, has built into it an egalitarian ethicopolitics. It harbors utopian notions about emancipation, freedom, and a better life (Wiegman). Hardt and Butler bear witness here. Opponents of cultural critique sometimes derisively label it the "victimization thesis," as if sexism, racism, colonialism, compulsory heterosexuality, and their interlocking dominations and antagonisms were no longer problems. Would it were so. To give up cultural critique strikes me as irresponsible and short-sighted.

It is worth stressing that Foucault does not talk about class, base/superstructure, or ideology. In place of Althusser's ideological state apparatuses, Foucault documents how modern social institutions develop productive docile bodies using "disciplines." Among the latter are surveillance, modes of objectification, tables of data and norms, records, hierarchies, examinations, and exercises. Practitioners of cultural critique are frequently, like Foucault, post-Marxist, if only because they do not believe in the ultimate triumph of the proletariat over the bourgeoisie (see, for example, Boltanski). What we have here is the Archie Bunker, hardhat, or Kansas phenomenon. Who today takes seriously the revolutionary radicalism of North American industrial workers? Saying farewell to this working class entails bidding adieu to some orthodox Marxist doctrines. For many critics, patriarchal and racial dominations appear at least as ancient and intractable as class struggle. Not surprisingly, there are practitioners of cultural critique who do not practice ideology critique, strictly speaking. I am not one of them. Rather I find ideology critique and cultural critique supplement one another. Neither one is dispensable. That is a crucial lesson of recent decades, the time of the rise of cultural studies in tandem with the corporate university and globalizing capitalism. In this context, critique usefully foregrounds alternatives and well as problems.

I treat intimate critique as an offshoot of cultural and ideology critique. I argue it merits separate consideration. By intimate critique I mean the analysis of personal emotions and lived experiences linked with everyday social, political, and economic forces and antagonisms. Take, for example, today's mounting anxieties concerning debt, or panic attacks stemming from multitasking, or insecurity over the spreading disposability of employees as well as resources and goods. Such calamities, large and small, affect me and my family plus friends and co-workers, as I made clear in Chapter 1. These common feelings, however individualized, clue us in to what is really going on (Freedman, Frey, Zauhar). They connect the emotional self to the larger surround of institutions, disciplines, and changing conventions. This is one way of historicizing the moment of reading. And it blends effectively with pleasure reading.[7] As a personalized fusion and extension of ideology and cultural critique, intimate critique constitutes an important survival skill for our time.

The tasks of critical reading

Recent critics advocating reparative, appreciative, uncritical, generous, surface, and restored close reading are misguided. Their programs lack balance and are lop-sided. I argue for including multifaceted critique along with close reading while encouraging pleasure reading. Such broadening is a matter of empowerment, arguably advocacy, but not indoctrination (Graff). Critical heuristics, I have found, can turn dogmatic principles into pragmatic tools. Encouraging and teaching pleasure reading for me means disabusing people of the idea that such reading is mindless, simple, or unworthy. Quite the contrary, research shows that personal "light reading" uses intricate sets of interpretive protocols. Close reading in my classrooms, as in many others if today's leading literature textbooks are any indication, involves stylistic analysis in a formalistic mode rooted in aesthetic appreciation of technique. The New Criticism lives on. My own mantra is technique is a test of sincerity, especially for majors in literature, rhetoric, and cultural studies. I promote units and courses in narrative theory, prosody, history of rhetoric, and stylistics. Along with textual analysis and critical evaluation, I make it a point to celebrate aesthetic beauty and to praise the best of its kind whatever the kind. What most interests me personally in ideology critique is systematic focus both on historical modes of

---

[7]Alan Jacobs mounts a nuanced and spirited defense of pleasure reading, but he omits consideration of critique, which he relegates to one sentence in his penultimate paragraph (149–150).

production like globalizing postmodernity and on institutions such as religion, education, and the family vis-à-vis the socioeconomic and political flows, frameworks, and antagonisms of the periods in question. Given today's intensifying capitalism, it's untimely to deemphasize or, worse yet, renounce ideology critique. As far as cultural critique, I, like many other critics, continue to find particularly rewarding in the classroom and in research questioning dynamics of race, gender, sexuality, and nationality. How, to take a case in point, do whiteness, femininity, queerness, national identity, and social class play out in 1920s US literary texts, for example, Hemingway's *The Sun Also Rises*, Fitzgerald's *The Great Gatsby*, Larsen's *Quicksand*, O'Neill's *All God's Chillun Got Wings*, Eliot's *The Waste Land*, and Hughes's *The Weary Blues*? You can teach a course on just such a question, as I have done. There should be no either/or between and among intimate critique, close reading, ideology critique, and cultural critique. But too often there is in recent calls to reclaim critical reading.

I realize that I have skirted an array of key topics related to critical reading today. I am assuming, for example, that infrastructures and circuits of literacy are in place. Here I mean not only primary and secondary schools; SAT, ACT, and other entrance exams; colleges and universities; but also publishers, bookstores (including Amazon.Books), libraries, family reading customs, study of scriptures, plus personal experience and street smarts. Furthermore, I'm not sure where in my account to situate unambiguously Do-It-Yourself reading practices, for instance, of consumer reports, loan documents, how-to guides, self-help manuals, diet books, Wikipedia articles, blogs, and so on. But clearly such reading involves flexible mixtures of interpretive modes.[8] It goes without saying, yet I perhaps haven't stressed it

---

[8]Compare "To be literate requires awareness of the parameters of engaging with books: slow, careful, often linear experiences that rely upon investments of attention, time, and money into words (that is, unless one skims, borrows, or Goggles the book). Meanwhile, Internet reading customs are consolidating around a different set of norms: quick, scattered, linked, multiple engagements with words, sounds, images, and design" (Juhasz). The protocols and conventions of Internet reading require ethnographic study (compare Radway). Juhasz simplifies here using a phalanx of the same old polar opposites in her hyped-up starkly binary account. In addition, she portrays literate reading as an investment more costly than Internet reading. But this observation strikes me as blinkered superficial accounting. See Baron for a more judicious account.

enough, reading is personal and interested, sometimes enchanting, sometimes risky, capable of changing lives for good and ill. It can be dangerous or life saving or both. This is the realm of criticism earlier theorists of reading labeled "response," often treating it as a distinct subcategory of uncritical reading or confessionalism, one step above superficial browsing. But phenomenologists and reader-response critics thankfully rectified that misapprehension decades ago (Bleich). Today neophenomenologists and others are in the helpful process of reconsidering the personal risks and rewards of reading. Intimate critique has a role here, as does pleasure reading. But such reconsiderations should not pit themselves against or demote critique.

I have not commented on a favorite of mine, namely excessive reading, that is, idiosyncratic, inventive, smart reading, the quirky countersigning commonly associated with Kenneth Burke, Harold Bloom, Jacques Derrida, Judith Butler, Slavoj Žižek, and others. (I examine Derrida as excessive reader in Chapter 6.) The tactics of these singular readers are both emulated and rapidly encapsulated in guidebooks. The latter can be useful for teaching students of literature, media, and culture. These prominent figures raise for fruitful consideration issues of overreading, underreading, and misreading; of meaning, ambiguity, and polysemy; and of the innumerable ways of contextualizing and transcoding works (Davis). As a group and singly, such critics are not immune to criticism, for example, ideology and cultural critique. The premium they put on creativity and wild innovation is in keeping with macho hyper capitalist values and market vanguardism. Excessive reading also fits very comfortably with the imperative of modernist as well as postmodern essay writing to be provocative, a highly esteemed value that often trumps the more conservative classical Enlightenment values of clarity, economy, and elegance, not to mention balance and truth. Insofar as these "deviant" critics have accrued cultural capital, they merit classroom discussion and critical inquiry on several additional counts, particularly assessing the dynamics of the celebrity status assigned to contemporary academostars.

I foresee a range of criticisms of my program for critical reading. It could be claimed, for example, it reduces criticism to a formula. Also it says nothing about proportionality, leaving the balance between close reading and critique unaddressed. It promotes the liberal values of multicultural diversity, critical fusion, and criticism of capitalism. Guilty as charged. Indeed, I recommend in the name of empowerment that students and practitioners use checklists, heuristic formulas, and tried and true techniques. My program deliberately does not assign fractions or percentages to its handful of designated critical methods and approaches, for it invariably comes down to case-by-case decisions. Without question, I remain critical of color- and gender-blind ideologies given the destructive racism, sexism, and heterosexism rampant in our world. Label it piety if you like, but it beats silence as a response. Capitalism has flaws, for example, chronic economic inequalities on evidence not only in everyday life, but also in literature, social discourse, and media. Let's address its weaknesses and strengths in our criticism. In the interests of pragmatism, flexibility, and broad scope, I advocate open-ended critical fusions. I am against reductionist programs for criticism such as formalist close reading only, exclusive art-for-art's sake aestheticism, selfless spiritualized phenomenology of unreading, or reader-centered existential phenomenology stripped of critique. They constitute throwbacks to modernist avant-gardism and fantasies of revitalized autonomy in an era when economics and politics enabled by media continue to seep into and reconfigure all spheres of life. Count me out on such nostalgic and defensive campaigns for purification.

Whether we treat ideology critique and close reading, intimate critique and cultural critique as heuristics or as personal articles of faith, I believe that in combining them there is a great deal of responsible work to do for literary and cultural analysts, teachers, and students. Unlike the four levels of patristic interpretation, neither hierarchy nor sequence needs to be adhered to with this hermeneutics blended for survival in our time.

4

Theory today and tomorrow

(Interview)

This interview was conducted by Professor Zhu Gang of Nanjing University, who specializes in American literature and critical theory. He is the Secretary General of the China Association for the Study of American Literature. Here he voices concerns of mainstream Chinese literary scholarship.

Zhu Gang: What is called "contemporary Western critical theory" by Chinese academics started in the 1960s, though "theoretical" approaches to literature could be traced back to the earlier period, for instance, formalism, psychoanalysis, and myth criticism. 1960s is a turning point in intellectual history, both in the West and in China. What is the most obvious connection, in your view, between the intellectual atmosphere of the 60s and the rise of theory thereafter?

Vincent B. Leitch: The 1960s mark a turning point in US culture for a handful of reasons. By the way, we date the "sixties" from 1964 to 1975, the dates of the passage of the Civil Rights Act and the complete withdrawal of US military troops from Vietnam. During these dozen years a great deal happened that positively impacted literary and cultural theory. It's complicated but there are some key landmarks.

The rise of the new social movements and cultural critique come first to my mind. Among these are women's rights, black power and ethnic rights, student's rights, gay rights, and Third World independence movements seeking the right to national sovereignty. These social and political groups—

often fractured within, some seeking assimilation into the mainstream, others wanting separatism and autonomy— mainly sought political recognition (rights). Typically, they put arguments for economic redistribution in second place and on hold. The tensions between rights and redistribution haunt criticism and politics to this day.

The women's rights movement gave us feminist theory, women's history, anthologies on women's literature, revaluation of women's genres like diaries and letters as well as innovative histories of the novel. Many hundreds of "forgotten" novels by women were rediscovered following the sixties. New ways of understanding were quickly developed: Elaine Showalter's *A Literature of Their Own* (1977) cast British women novelists as a subculture; Sandra Gilbert and Susan Gubar's *The Madwoman in the Attic* (1979) depicted female poets and novelists in terms of psychological disturbances generated by patriarchy (agoraphobia most memorably); Judith Fetterley's *The Resisting Reader* (1979) advocated cultural critique of misogynistic American classics from Washington Irving to Norman Mailer.

Parallel types of change occurred over ensuing decades, with wider visibility accorded African American, Native American, Hispanic American, Asian American, plus lesbigay and queer literatures. New courses, textbooks, programs, journals, academic press book series, and professional organizations have appeared, all legacies of the 1960s. I imagine Chinese scholars know all this, but it is worth remembering today. Cultural critique came to play an increasingly central role. The canon expanded. Along the way, literature became literatures. I recount the redefinition and reconfiguration of "literature" in a conference paper originally presented in Beijing: "Wenxue de quanquiuhua" ("Globalization of Literatures"), published in *Wenxue jingdian de jiangou, jiegou he changgou* (*The Construction, Deconstruction, and Reconstruction of the Literary Canon*), ed. Tao Dongfeng (Beijing: Peking University Press, 2007): 176–191. This paper forms the final chapter of my *Living with Theory*.

In other much more general terms, the universality of Enlightenment humanism—white male Western humanism—has been broadly replaced in the name of differences of race and ethnicity, of gender and sexuality, of minorities and nationalities. This marks the advent of postmodern multiculturalism, a battleground to this day.

The literature I studied and the methods I learned in the 1960s—shaped by modernist literary aestheticism and critical formalism—were overturned within 15 years. Yet the scrupulous methods of formalist close reading exhibit a remarkable staying power, as do the core canonical literary works. Arguments for restoration continue in the new century.

Other new literary and cultural theory stems from the 1960s. I have not mentioned 1960s and 1970s US imperialism and postcolonial theory, plus cultural studies in response to the proliferation of mass media and popular culture. Nor have I touched on the 1970s rise of free-market capitalism, politically organized Christian fundamentalism, and many backlash phenomena. The way I see it, the impact of the sixties, broadly construed, continues unfolding in the twenty-first century.

ZG: Why do you think cultural issues like race, ethnicity, and gender should have become major concerns of literature in recent decades? Do we have more urgent concerns than those focusing on the postcolonial and the homosexual?

VBL: US society and universities have since the 1960s opened the doors to women and people of "color." Gays and lesbians have had some success in getting fair and equal treatment in legal and political as well as social and cultural arenas. American imperial aspirations and ventures continue to deplete our resources and to vex intellectuals, particularly those with roots in other nations and those with cosmopolitan outlooks. So academic research and teaching have reflected the concerns of these groups and activist movements. The majority white population is decreasing in size. The US is undeniably a multicultural society despite the fantasies of nativists. The UK, France, and Germany are all dealing with similar issues of minorities.

The publish-or-perish imperative of scholarship has permeated not only major research universities since the 1960s, but also baccalaureate and Master's awarding institutions. Doctoral students increasingly try to get "hot topics" for their dissertations and conference papers to be competitive in the fierce job market. Race, class, and gender analyses along with postcolonial and queer theory suit the trends in the profession for publication and promotion. Also consumer capitalism is addicted to bigger, better, and the new. The hunger for the new is voracious in society and in academia. Market vanguardism is alive and well in the university, including literature departments. Multicultural theory fills that need too.

ZG: You have promoted recent critical trends moving towards cultural studies. However, cultural studies seems to have experienced difficulties, for instance, the close down of CCCS at the University of Birmingham in the UK. There is also resistance to "culturalization" of literature in China where a number of critics are arguing for a return to literature itself.

VBL: Cultural studies has specific histories and profiles in each nation. US cultural studies is separate from Australian, British, Canadian, etc. (Groden; Turner). At the moment, US cultural studies has four or five identities: it is an approach or method; a disciplinary wing; a new discipline (sometimes a department); a dominant research paradigm; a movement. This situation is quite different from the UK.

With the cultural wars of the past three decades in the US came calls to restore the canon of Great Books, renounce "political correctness" (race-class-gender analyses), and return to literature. This ongoing battle summons "literature itself." In the US that special phrase resurrects the mid-century formalism of early Cold War New Criticism, with its three infamous taboos against the intentional fallacy (biographical research), the affective fallacy (reader response), and the heresy of paraphrase (worldly themes). As a New Critic, you are instructed—commanded—to focus on the work and not on the writer's biography (intentions), nor on the reader's response (affects), nor on the paraphrasable meaning of the text. This last point means the autonomous "literary object" must not be reduced to or compete with philosophy, theology, law, science, psychology, politics, etc. The "literariness" of literature, its distinctive aesthetic features, distinguishes it for a formalist from other disciplines. It merits an academic department of its own, a secure home in the university. Moreover, the formalist claim of autonomy for literature descends from the Kantian antiutilitarian Enlightenment tradition as defensively manifested during the 1930s against the bad politicizations of art. Formalism today remains a conservative political defense against the deaestheticization of art. All that said, the concept "literature itself" carries a great deal of baggage. Handle with care is my advice.

Instead of seeing the current culturalization of literature as a threat, I believe it performs a rescue operation not only from dogmatic formalism but also from the rise of popular culture with its antiquation of literature. Against formalist strictures, cultural studies forwards vital postformalist protocols of method. For instance, when analyzing a work or phenomenon, a cultural critic seeks to examine the cultural circuits (production, distribution, consumption). That opens research to biographical and historical inquiry as well as audience response and institutional analysis. It violates the New Critical fallacies, but without renouncing close reading. There are many more modes of close reading than literary formalism. It is worth recalling here that by the late 1960s formalist close reading had become repetitive, predictable, deadening. That is based on my personal experience. In its wake theory and cultural studies have opened new and exciting—life-enhancing—frontiers for research and publication plus, of course, for teaching.

By the way, there are a dozen or more identifiable antitheory factions as well as lone individuals in the US who call for a "return to literature." Perhaps it's similar in China.

ZG: What difference does theory make to the study of literature? Could we simply read literary texts without reading or thinking in theory? Could we return to a time when critics did only criticism and were unaffected by theoretical considerations? Is theory only a decoration of the ivory tower, inaccessible to general readership? Or is it mainly a proof of sophistication, a pre-requisite for the MA thesis and PhD dissertation?

VBL: How to define "theory" and its many facets? "Theory" designates the broad field of contemporary schools and movements. It also signifies principles, procedures, and methods, plus self-reflection. In addition, it labels the toolbox of useful devices, terms, and concepts employed by readers and critics, now and in the past. It names, moreover, professional common sense—what every specialist knows and what goes without saying. In this important sense, everyone has theory. It sometimes means poststructuralism, frequently nicknamed high theory or French theory. To complicate matters, theory designates the historically new discourse or field—a postmodern phenomenon—that assembles and fuses modern disciplines and subdisciplines into a hybrid compound of literary criticism, linguistics, anthropology, psychoanalysis, philosophy, sociology, history, and political economy. As its critics point out, most contemporary theory is linked with standpoint epistemology, social constructionism, cultural relativism, and popular culture, so it is very much a postmodern formation.

Now to answer your question head on, literary criticism is entangled with theory in various senses. Criticism is inconceivable without theory, I would argue. Even the non-academic reader relies on theory—knowingly as well as unwittingly. He believes he knows what literature is; why characters make decisions; where men, women, and children properly belong; how to understand people, society, the world; what constitutes well-made as well as poorly constructed literary plots and good literary styles; the conventions of genre. There is no escape from theory for readers. The wish to be before or after theory, to bury theory, is an angry fantasy. It defines theory too narrowly as a political extension of the new social movements of the 1960s, or as French (post)structuralism, or as this ambitious and unmanageable crossdisciplinary field. Those are the usual suspects—the enemies familiar from the ongoing US cultural wars. Yet theory is more than all that.

In the contemporary American university, theory functions as an agent of the new and the cutting edge in the majority of subfields and periods of literary studies. It is a ticket to publication, employment, promotion. It has become especially since the 1970s the air literary academics breathe; it sustains the profession and the mission of the research-oriented university. Not surprisingly, there has arisen the counterindustry of antitheory. In other words, people and projects are defined and positioned in relation to theory. I hasten to add that there is plenty of bad theory (ill-informed, wrong-headed, poorly argued, dogmatic, narrow, mechanical, opaque, jargon-ridden, insensitive, affected, gimmicky, narcissistic, etc.).

ZG: Derrida is the father of deconstruction, against which all the other post-structuralist perspectives on literature define themselves. But we know Derrida changed a lot during the last ten years or so of his life. You have read Derrida quite comprehensively. How do you account for this change we find in him? Or is it the same Derrida, but we read him differently?

VBL: Jacques Derrida published many books over the course of forty years, beginning in the mid-1960s. None of these works is systematic philosophy as in Kant or Hegel. Most were written in response to situations. They are often haphazard. They frequently meander. It's a sprawling corpus.

Starting in the late 1980s, Derrida turned for the first time more fully and openly to ethics and politics. We can speculate on his motives. There were, for example, long-standing pressures on him to address politics, going back to the early 1970s. In 1987, deconstruction was put under special suspicion by the revelation of Paul de Man's links to World War II German fascism. Let's recall that de Man was Derrida's colleague and friend at Yale University as well as the leading American deconstructor of the time. Also Martin Heidegger, often favorably referenced by Derrida, had obvious ties to Nazism. What else? The Union of Soviet Socialist Republics went out of existence rapidly starting in 1989, which facilitated the rampant global spread of radical free-market capitalism during the 1990s. As a man of the left, Derrida sensed a threat from triumphant US neoliberalism to France and the European Union. He began to write about these and other current events until his death, becoming a politically engaged public intellectual like other theorists of the time.

A friend of mine, Professor Steven Mailloux then at the University of California-Irvine where Derrida taught for two decades during several weeks each spring, told me in March 2004 that Derrida was sick and would not be teaching that spring. The prognosis was negative. Spontaneously and in mourning, I started composing a retrospective and planning a graduate seminar on Late Derrida. In May, I spent a few weeks in Paris obtaining late Derrida materials. By early October, after eight months of work, I sent my retrospective to the journal *Critical Inquiry* just a few days before Derrida's death. The editor took my title, "Late Derrida," and organized a special issue on the topic (also released as a book), both published in 2007 by the University of Chicago Press. In that work, I sum up Derrida's late politics and lay out my critique of it.

Looking back now from the vantage point of ten years, the key books in Derrida's late works on politics for me remain his innovative *Specters of Marx* (1993) especially and *Rogues* (2003), along with the extensive information-packed interviews in his *For What Tomorrow* (2001) and the provocative one in *Philosophy in a Time of Terror* (2003).

But as far as both the reception and the multifaceted critical legacy of Derrida go, they have been from the start immensely productive and contentious in the US. His work positively impacted centrist as well as leftist American deconstructive theory, as with the careers of J. Hillis Miller and Gayatri Chakravorty Spivak. It contributed to African American and Native American theory (Henry Louis Gates and Gerald Vizenor), plus feminism, postcolonial theory, psychoanalysis, and queer theory, most notably in the work of Barbara Johnson, Homi Bhabha, Eve Sedgwick, and Judith Butler. It helped buttress structuralism and semiotics as in the instance of Jonathan Culler, and also speech-act theory in the projects of Shoshana Felman, for example. Beyond literary studies, Derridean deconstruction fruitfully impacted American philosophy, theology, law, and cultural studies. I hasten to add that the "late Derrida" maintained his interest in literary figures, publishing a half dozen books of literary criticism during the last 15 years of his life. Yet my favorite literary exegeses remain those textual analyses in his early book *Dissemination*, particularly the extended critique there of Plato's dialogues.

ZG: You published *American Literary Criticism from the 1930s to the 1980s* in 1988. A new edition appeared in 2010. When you revised, what changes or corrections did you make to previous chapters and what did you add for the theory of very recent years?

VBL: In the first edition of 1988, I offered 13 chapters covering the main schools and movements (Marxism, New Criticism, Chicago School, New York Intellectuals, Myth Criticism, Phenomenology and Existentialism, Hermeneutics, Reader-Response Criticism, Structuralism and Semiotics, Poststructuralism and Deconstruction, Feminist Criticism, Black Aestheticism, and Cultural Criticism). Incidentally, I do not consider psychoanalysis a school or a movement like the others: it has a pervasive and continuous history since the 1920s. So I weave it into the accounts of the schools and movements, ultimately giving it more space than all the others. In any case, I added a new chapter to the second edition. It discusses New Historicism, Postcolonial Criticism, Queer Theory, Ethnic Criticism (especially Chicano, Native American, and Asian American), and Cultural Studies. I also updated the earlier chapters. The biggest change was recontexualizing the Cold War era, which had not ended until 1989–1991 with the collapse of the Soviet Union.

Part of my argument in the second edition is that the schools and movements method of organization does not work for the twenty-first century. Nor does it work for earlier centuries. What we have since the 1990s is the ongoing disaggregation of the field of literary criticism and theory into "studies" areas (many many dozens of them). I am thinking of transatlantic studies, whiteness studies, body studies, popular culture studies, narrative studies, animal studies, performance studies, etc. Most of these subfields operate under the extremely broad banner of cultural studies. So another part of my argument is that the field has become vast, disorganized, and not masterable. A proper microhistory of recent decades would in my view have to be collectively constructed and narrated. This would be a new mode of writing the history of theory.

In narrating the history of American literary criticism from 1988 to 2010, I found as significant as the new fin-de-siècle schools and movements and the rise of many new studies areas a set of related events. Here I have in mind the fall of Paul de Man; the debates about postmodernity and globalization; the culture wars and the reemergence of the public intellectual; plus the rise of the corporate "university of excellence" with the massive casualization of professors and the proliferation of student debt.

ZG: As the general editor of the *Norton Anthology of Theory and Criticism*, what are the principles and the assumptions you hold in compiling such a volume?

VBL: During the two-year revision process for our second edition, the five editors and I went through a half dozen overlapping phases or rounds. No one ever talks about this process so I want briefly to shed light on it in order to reveal principles, assumptions, etc. To start with, let me mention numbers. We dropped about 20 of the original 148 figures. Then we lightly trimmed selections from 12 existing figures. After that it was swaps and enhancements affecting 15 figures. For examples of the latter, we cut 10 pages from Derrida's lengthy "Plato's Pharmacy," while adding that many pages from his *Specters of Marx*. We enhanced the materials from Pierre Bourdieu with a piece from his *Rules of Art* on the social status of various literary genres to supplement the introduction to his *Distinction*. To the introduction of Edward Said's *Orientalism*, we added a section from his *Culture and Imperialism*, which offers an exemplary postcolonial reading of Jane Austen's fiction in relation to the British Empire. In the next, the fourth round of revision, we chose new figures and texts—15 in all. Among them are Franco Moretti, Judith Halberstam, Paul Gilroy, Lisa Lowe, Andrew Ross, N. Katherine Hayles, and Slavoj Žižek. A fifth round involved "reconsiderations," that is, a few last-minutes final cuts and restorations. For instance, we discovered we could not have an anthology on the history of theory and criticism without Matthew Arnold's "Function of Criticism at the Present Time." We initially thought we could simply drop it.

By the way, the *Norton* is the only theory anthology put together by a team. Most are edited by one person. The team has members from two generations and no one party line. It tries to be broadly representative of the interests of literature professors working in the US and UK. The publisher—W. W. Norton (an employee-owned firm protected from buyouts)— surveyed in a detailed manner 200 users of the original 2001 anthology. That produced many recommendations for change while representing the broad concerns of theory teachers. The second edition has new thematic foci on ethics and literary criticism, globalization, new historicisms, and antitheory. We also have new translations and editions of canonical texts by Plato, Augustine, du Bellay, Sidney, Vico, Kant, Benjamin, etc. Our last round of revision, the sixth, involved us in selecting four non-Western representative theory texts from contemporary Arabic (Adūnis), Chinese (Li Zehou), Indian (C. D. Narasimhaiah), and Japanese (Karantani Kōjin).

To address your question in theory terms rather than narrative retrospection, the criteria for choosing a text include some combination of significance, influence, uniqueness, poignancy, pertinence, readability, teachability, length, and resonance. This mantra is my editorial touchstone, dating from the early planning stages. In deciding on canonical as well as cutting-edge contemporary selections, we juggle these criteria. Another principle is that we prefer complete or self-contained texts (essays, chapters, poems, prefaces, letters) rather than snippets. Also at least half of the six editors have to agree on including each selection. And of course our primary readerships—undergraduate and graduate literature students—shape our sense of readability and teachability. Last but not least, the criterion of "resonance" means we seek to create mosaics not strings of isolated pearls. We are on the lookout for thematic clusters, like ethics and literary criticism, theory of globalization, new historicisms, etc. It is a matter of attending to arguments and putting them in touch with one another across the headnotes and in a multifaceted Alternative Table of Contents.

ZG: Some of the critical concerns in the West have become global, such as postcolonial and environment issues. Has this happened, as far as you can see, the other way round? Have issues of developing countries become literary concerns of Western critics?

VBL: The terms of this question pose a problem. The difficulty arises with the concept of the West versus the non-West. All across the West—in the US, UK, France, and Germany, for example—there reside large non-Western "Third World" populations within developed countries, increasingly so since World War II. The concerns of these populations have infiltrated mainstream cultural as well as political agendas of advanced Western societies. Among the most obvious topics of contention coming from non-Western populations within the contemporary West are the status of second languages, religions, dress, minority literatures, and separatist versus integrationist philosophies. Other issues include differences between generations of immigrants, nondiscriminatory public education, racism, citizenship, equal rights. What else? Most notably, economic opportunity and justice, that is, fair distribution of resources (food, shelter, clothing, water, money, energy, credit, etc.).

Insofar as North American indigenous groups (550 Native American tribes, for instance) remain internal non-Western colonies, they constitute special cases of developing nations residing inside developed ones.

There is more. On the literary level, the very recent spread of globalized language-based poetics within the developed Western countries injects the lifeworlds of developing countries inside Western university literature curricula. I am referring to Anglophone, Francophone, and Hispanophone literatures where the conditions and concerns of Africa, Asia, Latin America, and the Middle East come front and center. On the one hand, such formations appear like alien viruses but, on the other, they are subject to the hegemonic order. Here we come face to face with the mixed blessings of cultural recognition. Many English Departments today teach Anglophone literature alongside national literatures (American, Irish, English, etc.). French and Spanish departments reflect analogous realignments.

ZG: You have talked in recent pieces about your own life experiences, which seem to have made your personal commitment to theory appear quite natural and even inevitable. This personal involvement in a social and historical context congenial to theory is shared by many established theoreticians of your age. However, as the personal experience of and the social context for the young generation must be very different from yours, the inevitability of theory does not seem to exist today. This relates to the question of the justification of theory. So on what grounds do you believe that "theory still matters"?

VBL: My fusion of theorizing and life writing derives from several sources, namely feminism, the academic memoir boom starting in the 1990s, and the premium put on everyday life by cultural studies. bell hooks provides a well-known exemplary blend of close reading, ideology critique, cultural critique, and personalized theory, that is, intimate critique. I come from her generation.

As is so frequently the case with the arts, generations matter. The generation of early American baby boomers born between World War II and the Vietnam War came of age during the 1960s. We experienced the transitions from critical formalism to poststructuralism to cultural studies that distinguish the closing decades of the twentieth century. This period was marked by the triumph of popular culture, the expansion of literary canons, and the proliferation of literary and critical approaches. It was followed by backlashes against the new social movements, secularism, and the Welfare State. And it culminated with the declaration of a New World Order, confirming the hegemony of radical laissez-faire capitalism and the resurgence especially after 9/11 of American militarized imperialism. 24/7 proliferating media increasingly magnified all these events, particularly the Great Recession starting in 2008. No doubt, this constitutes a very particular generational experience.

While I believe the experience of each generation, each intellectual cohort, is singular, there is much continuity also. Tradition lives on not only as vestigial but as dominant. Education counts on that. The generation of older professors ahead of me and the two generations of younger professors behind me have much in common. Our differences seem less weighty, however intensely felt. We share an archive plus a professional and cultural unconscious.

Still, there is more to consider. Most literature departments in the US offer three standard *theory* courses. They have been doing so for a century: History of Theory, Modern Theory, and Introduction to Theory. History covers Plato and Aristotle to Marx and Nietzsche. Modern usually means twentieth and now twenty-first century (from Freud, Saussure, Eliot, and Bahktin to Fanon, Foucault, Said, and Jameson to hooks, Butler, and Žižek). Introduction to Theory generally explores key concepts and terms such as genre, authorship, interpretation, canon, discourse, representation, modernity, subjectivity, narrativity, etc. When I was an undergraduate student, I took both History of Theory and Modern Theory. There was no introductory course at my university. One picked up the basic terms and concepts in the required literary survey courses, genre and period offerings, and great writers courses. In any case, my argument is that theory permeates the literature curricula informally as well as formally. It is inevitable. I don't see this changing.

What I do foresee changing is whether theory courses and questions will be required or optional, not to mention popular or unpopular with students. In order for theory to be life enhancing, productive, and popular for students as well as professors, they must have a personal stake in its issues, figures, texts, movements. Of that I have little doubt. But even if the popularity of theory declines and it becomes the possession of a coterie, that has its advantages too.

There is nowadays a market in theory, which your question suggests. "Investors take care where you invest your resources." This is how we talk and think today, emphasizing short terms and big returns. So I continue to proclaim: things look good on the theory market, both for today and tomorrow. Theory provides cultural and professional as well as personal capital.

ZG: You have been teaching theory and literature courses for years. What is the relevance of theory to literature, especially for undergraduate literature courses? In a much-changed world, how will you convince young students that theory still has its value?

VBL: I recently offered a course in cultural theory that examined the closing decades of the twentieth century. The course got excellent enrollment: students were very interested evidently. What I did was focus single-mindedly on blockbusters—complex and influential books (famous contemporary classics)—that I judged to be life-changing. This is one way to make theory of value to students. You broaden and unsettle their worlds. You get them to grapple with pressing critical questions and problems. You have them engage celebrated major works.

This course was designed primarily for upper-level undergraduate literature majors, although five graduate students enrolled along with the 15 undergraduates. We explored bell hooks, *Outlaw Culture*; Frantz Fanon, *The Wretched of the Earth*; Edward Said, *Orientalism*; Michel Foucault, *Discipline and Punish* and *History of Sexuality*, vol. 1; Judith Butler, *Gender Trouble*; Fredric Jameson, *Postmodernism, or the Cultural Logic of Late Capitalism*; and Michael Hardt and Antonio Negri, *Empire*. Students were required to write critical review essays and take turns leading discussions on these works. Insofar as the matrix or main paradigm nowadays for US academic literary studies derives from major texts of cultural theory, this course provided students detailed familiarity with the topics, concepts, and questions of most concern to teachers and scholars. It also provided them memorable reading experiences. The course earned unusually high student-teacher evaluations.

When I recently taught a second iteration of this course, I dropped the second Foucault book and the Butler text and added Jameson's *The Political Unconscious*, Žižek's *The Sublime Object of Ideology*, and Halberstam's *Female Masculinity*. It's a matter of experimenting. Also I profited here from students' recommendations, which I always solicit.

In addition to teaching literary texts and literary history—which I do regularly—we literary scholars, critics, and theorists have other obligations to students, graduate as well as undergraduate. In our programs we must inform them about the history and structure of our discipline's concepts, taxonomies, and main concerns, plus the reigning critical approaches and theories of the day. Moreover, we have to teach students how to not only recognize and apply, but also assess and criticize contending critical approaches, whether formalist, deconstructive, cultural studies, or Marxist, psychoanalytical, feminist, postcolonial, etc. Also we have an obligation to make them aware of the vital explosion of subdisciplines and new fields of the past few decades. And insofar as students, especially graduate students, frequently wonder "what is going on?" and "what is the latest thing?," we have an additional obligation to help professionalize students as critics and to provoke while satisfying their curiosity about their field.

5

Theory crossroads

(A conversation)

This engaged conversation was initiated by Daniel Morris, Professor of English at Purdue University and specialist in modern American literature and culture.

Daniel Morris: Your 2008 Blackwell Manifesto is called *Living with Theory*. A cunning title. It could mean a grudging acceptance, as in "OK, I'm an old school literature guy, but, I give in, I'll learn to apply bits and pieces of theory in my survey of canonical masters." Or, it could be a kind of virus, an affliction: "Darn, I've got this theory bug, but, I'm learning to live with it." Or, and this is what I assume to be the Leitch approach: Knowing theory has somehow changed or enabled or informed your daily life. Could you reflect on how you "live" with theory? Can you ever turn the "theory head" off and, to commercialize this conversation, "Just Do It"? You mention in your book how even your decision to wear a suit and tie to class is a meaningful, a theoretical, gesture, one that allows you to go undercover as a subversive "dangerous professor." What is it like for you "living with theory"? It must inform the way you read the paper in the morning, the food you eat, the way you watch TV, the car you drive, your interpersonal relations. I guess it could be described as a bit of a viral disease, this living with theory!

Vincent B. Leitch: Let me respond several indirect ways. When Fredric Jameson discusses the features of postmodern culture in his landmark *Postmodernism, or the Cultural Logic of*

Late Capitalism, he mentions architecture, film, music, food, literature, art, philosophy and, of course, political economy. The pastiche at the heart of the postmodern aesthetic, he suggests, recurs across the different domains of culture, high and low, from the 1950s onwards. Here are some examples from me. Wolfgang Puck's putting Asian-Style shrimp on Italian pizza in 1970s Los Angeles resembles the sampling of rappers, who at the same time are mixing and matching odd musical tracks, which is what some leading LANGUAGE poets are also doing. The same goes for the neo-expressionist painters, especially David Salle, whose zones of collaged images copied from pornography, popular culture, and later aristocratic interiors jostle against one another on the same untextured matte canvas. Gene splicing and recombinant DNA come to mind as technoscientific analogues. The rise of the assemblage as the dominant new genre of contemporary art substantiates the implosion of borders and fusions typical of the postmodern era. This is the period when literary and cultural critics start talking about intertextuality, deconstructed hierarchies, interpretive communities, multiple subject positions, heteroglossia, and hybridity. We label it "theory," a postmodern formation. And yes it's gone viral. Today the typical Web 2.0 page mixes formats derived from newspapers, videos, radio, graphic designs, and advertisements. But theory or no theory, such fusions are happening. Well, so, my point is the disaggregation and pastiche characteristic of postmodern times might be spotted anywhere in the culture. Other instances: rock operas, channel surfing, the mixed family, the family of 157 mutual funds offered by Vanguard, the *Cremaster Cycle* of Matthew Barney. We need to account for these phenomena. Theory, itself a fusion, does that effectively.

I can make my claim another more historicist way. The autonomies of art, science, religion, and politics characteristic of modernity have been collapsing all around us, for good and ill. The autonomy of art seems now a distant dream of the historical avant-gardes. Likewise with the ideal of separation of church and state. What kind of criticism best responds to such neo-baroque historical mutations? Cultural studies, I believe. Itself a hodgepodge—a postmodern interdiscipline—it consists of customizable mixtures of sociology, anthropology, history, Marxism, media studies, gender studies, popular culture studies, and so on. This kind of theory responds to its time.

Let me come at this question from one last angle. The notion of "everyday life," fundamental for cultural studies and theory, requires of critical inquiry investigation into the quotidian, the vernacular, the commonplace. No restrictions. Now, if you add to that the ancient philosophical admonition to self-reflection, you end up with a criticism and theory extending into your personal everyday life: eating, dressing, reading, going and coming, working, maintaining relationships, watching television, managing money, exercising, sleeping, etc. This version of "theory," self-reflective contemporary cultural studies—a postmodern concoction par excellence—takes to a limit the venerable idea that the "unexamined life is not worth living." It brings it home (an example of the implosion of the domestic and public spheres). It's a mixture of intimate personal criticism with cultural and ideological critique rooted in analysis and meditation. This is what, I believe, living with theory involves for our time and place. The Do-It-Yourself vernacular version of living with theory is 24/7 "street smarts."

DM: I hope this question doesn't sound too "New Critical," but I notice how often you consciously confront the ambiguities, paradoxes, and contradictions in your own work as a theorist. I'm thinking, for example, of your important comments on the current state of the corporate university. As an endowed distinguished professor, you exist as something of a "Brahmin"—one of those with what Stanley Aronowitz calls "the last good job in America"—but you hail from a working-class background and in the context of the downsizing and casualizing of much of a professoriate whose working conditions crumble around you. You describe the current situation in academia as a reflection of a postmodern condition of "disaggregation," and yet your major scholarly contributions have come in the form of crystal clear maps, and you the organizer without fellow of often wildly disparate texts ranging from Aristotle to Žižek. You are a profound critic of a consumer society in which "the new" is fetishized and a 24/7 work ethic is promoted, and yet perhaps more than anyone I know you have devoted much of your adult life to producing books and textbooks that feed the desire of publishers and readers alike to know where to look for the cutting edge. You are a first-class theory head and yet in places I get the sense of your soft spot for literature, poetry especially, as when you critique Mikhail Bakhtin for his blindness to poets such as Whitman who are every bit as heteroglossic as are the Russian novelists. Are such paradoxes in the category of "of course, what do you expect in an all-consuming postmodern era"? Do you struggle with these paradoxes, or accept them as inherent contradictions of our time? Do these contradictions weigh on you, encouraging you to alter your stances, work habits, critical approaches?

VBL: I don't see any contradiction between the disaggregation characteristic of postmodern culture and clear, well-organized maps of it. This reminds me of that useful formula from cybernetics: information overload equals pattern recognition. Perhaps more pertinent models here would be contemporary theories of fractals, chaos, and catastrophe, all seeking the underlying mathematical order of apparent disorder.

On the question of the late capitalist market obsession with the new and my profiting off that demand, there is a paradoxical relation. My books and courses (re)package the newest theory in manageable formats and profit in doing so. At the same time I empower my students and readers. It's a mission. As a socialist, I want changes to the current extremist free-market political economy. On the day that I am responding to you during the Great Recession, my brother is long-term unemployed without health insurance. His benefits ran out long ago, except for food stamps. My sister lives off a skimpy Social Security check with her ailing husband in a house subsidized by one of her children. They lost their house through bank foreclosure. There can be a better world. But the terms and conditions of engagement in our current neoliberal hegemonic order are more or less clearly set. One negotiates with them as an insider-outsider. In a way, the task of any critic is paradoxical, weighing the good against the bad. T. W. Adorno once memorably characterized the contemporary cultural critic as a hired hand of the culture.

For me there is no contradiction or tension between doing cultural theory and loving literature. Antitheorists perceive a contradiction. Yet most theorists don't. Especially in the 1980s, there was animosity between these two camps at the time of the rise of theory in the US university. That tension has more or less subsided in most places. But it can and does flare up at a moment's notice. I have never stopped teaching literature, which I enjoy. I did vow very early in my career not to publish any more literary criticism, having published a few articles on poetry. Instead, I dedicated myself to "theory" conceived as a postmodern specialty. Starting in 1970, the declining "job market" prompted intensified career planning, especially pre-occupation with the curriculum vitae, its fullness, quality, and coherence. I decided to build a profile as a theorist, with no second area as backup. That was a professional calculation driven by the genuine passion of a convert. I imagine immunologists, biochemists, and computer scientists of the time followed a similar path out of general medicine, chemistry, and mathematics into their emerging new fields, without renouncing the traditional disciplines.

But, yes, there is a contradiction between my starting point and my present position. However, it is not what it appears. I have written about my transformation from a poorly paid assistant professor at a small private Baptist university to an endowed professor at a public research university. Believe it or not, I applied for and received government food stamps in the earliest days in protest against low faculty salaries. But my career provides an image of class mobility. In my first steady academic job, obtained after receiving my PhD and after doing one year of postdoctoral teaching as an Interim Assistant Professor of Humanities, I spent thirteen years at this Southern liberal arts Christian university of middling rank. Married with two children, I managed to complete two books and "publish my way out of there." So I am an example for others of how you can publish yourself out of a lower-tier institution. The idea of meritocracy lives on. American culture desperately clutches to that idea, a core ideology, no matter what. For doctoral students these days, I am an example of what a successful career looks like—good compensation, low teaching load, ample research assistance, lots of publications, big title, international travel. But given the actual labor situation of the post-Welfare State corporate university, all endowed professors are positioned as Brahmins amongst untouchables. The corporate university, a pyramid, has exorbitantly multiplied the number of temporary workers and added some endowed (i.e., privatized) professorships in tandem. Nowadays there are so few tenure-track full-time jobs in academic humanities teaching and so many job candidates and insecure casualized temporary workers. It's an era of disposable workers. The contradiction I have most in mind comes in this: percentage-wise very few academics will publish themselves out of lower-tier institutions, and even fewer will attain distinguished research chairs. But note: this contradiction comes at the level of the corporate university system, however much it is lived personally and singularly.

DM: You began your studies as a traditional English literature major in the 1960s and 1970s, trained in the New Criticism. You taught in what sounds like a quite traditional "Great Books" style program as your first job, a one-year postdoctoral position, at the University of Florida right out of grad school. As your past comments about your work as editor of the *Norton Anthology of Theory and Criticism* indicate, your knowledge of classical rhetoric is impressive. In a previous question, I mentioned your obvious admiration for poetry, as demonstrated in your essay detailing the contemporary poetry scene in *Living with Theory*.

My question has to do with generational differences, backgrounds, trainings, and emphases as pertains to the relation between literature and theory. How would you compare your training and background with your experience of how theory-oriented graduate students and newly minted

PhDs are trained today? From your comments on the several stages of job hiring over the last three decades, it sounds like you feel theory is "winning," but in something of a covert manner, as literature departments, inherently conservative, continue to hire in traditional periods, literary genres, and national literatures, but more or less demand a consciously held theoretical expertise among new hires. Do you feel this merging of theory and literature in contemporary hiring practices takes us full circle, producing younger generations of scholars who, like you, represent knowledge bases that include theory and literature? Is this for you a healthy development, when compared, for example, to the more rigidly demarcated lines drawn between theory and literature during the "culture wars" of the 1980s and 1990s? Would you contrast today's hybridization of theory/lit scholars to your progression (or conversion) from literature to theory, a process that required you to self-educate in part by seeking out alternative educational venues such as NEH seminars and the School for Criticism and Theory? Do you feel your strong training in a conservative tradition of literary study has proven helpful—or perhaps inhibiting—to you as a scholar, editor, teacher, and mentor, even as you have strongly critiqued the limitations and blind spots of New Critical training and a theory of canons as little more than the pantheon of Great Male Authors?

VBL: During my student days in the 1960s, American literary criticism entailed scrupulous stylistic analysis typically focused on short canonical poetic texts and passages. It required painstaking attention to aesthetic detail and pattern in well-made works, that is, formalist close reading. I remain grateful for this analytical training and the immersion in canonical literature. It is empowering and gratifying, I have found, not only with literature but also with painting and music. Careful, patient looking and listening informed by tradition can be immensely rewarding. I always teach students the importance and techniques of textual explication of individual works in the context of tradition. However, I do emphasize that there are many modes and styles of close reading and many strands of tradition, with the latter subject to revisions.

The limitations that come along with strict formalist criticism became increasingly suffocating for me. I have in mind the infamous strictures against meaning (art for art's sake and the heresy of paraphrase), biographical inquiry (the intentional fallacy), and personal response (the affective fallacy). But most vexing was the general taboo on "extrinsic" concerns. I had an adverse reaction early in my career to all this dogma. Mind you, I sympathize with the depoliticizing-aestheticizing move of formalism during the interwar years when socialist realism became a government-sponsored compulsory literary mode and when so-called "degenerate literature" was being burned in public squares by organized authoritarian political forces. It's strategic formalism. I accept that. It had the effect of protecting literature, particularly non-realist avant-garde works, from extirpation and extermination. Such circumstances help explain the long-standing purifying mentality of formalism, too often accompanied by a quasi-religious effort to separate art from worldliness.

The rise of theory during the past generation, the postmodern era, has had a range of notable effects. Theory in all its plurality has penetrated every academic literary specialty and subspecialty more or less thoroughly. I think of this progression as Theory Incorporated. Less completely in Medieval compared to Modernist literary studies, I observe. I am thinking here mainly of the publication apparatus (conferences, reviews, articles, books, grant proposals). Most publications explicitly indicate theoretical affiliations and employ tools of theory. In that sense, they are placeable, identifiable. In addition, theory runs through many literature courses more or less continuously and explicitly. Unlike during my graduate training, students nowadays pick up theory both in literature and in separate theory courses. But this disparate immersion can be a hit-or-miss process. The solution: graduate students can do a major or minor, a certificate, or a self-directed program in theory. None of these conditions and options existed when I was a student.

DM: We are conducting this conversation in the wake of the extraordinarily mediated death and burial of pop icon Michael Jackson. The range of responses in various print, TV, and online media is dizzying. A journalism professor from the University of Pennsylvania has criticized the judgment of journalists, particularly the major news networks, for covering this story wall to wall while such stories as the passage of a (watered down) legislative bill on global warming, an international summit, arms talks between the US and Russia, a US Supreme Court nomination involving the first Hispanic and one of the first women, revolutionary movements in Iran, and other crises such as in China took a back seat. Leading black intellectuals like Cornel West and Michael Eric Dyson have framed Michael Jackson in the context of the nineteenth-century Romantic genius and as a troubled modernist "master," likening Jackson to Vincent van Gogh. Jackson gave others pleasure because he couldn't himself experience pleasure, they argued. As expected, Fox TV reactionaries such as Bill O'Reilly have taken the opportunity to bash Jackson as a selfish drug addict and pedophile. Others have seen Jackson's death as a symbol of an age where the easy access to prescription drugs has become a national epidemic. For me the most interesting analysis of Jackson has been in placing him as a postmodern "self," a metamorphic cyborg performative self that upsets essentialist conceptions of race, gender, and sexuality. If you were currently teaching a course on contemporary theory or cultural studies, would you see "Michael Jackson" as a useful site to discuss these and other responses? Do you have a personal take on Michael Jackson, the media frenzy surrounding his death, and, in general, what seems at this time to be (even by recent standards) a mainstream media obsession with the indiscretions of celebrities?

VBL: At the moment I am responding to your question, it has been a short time since the unexpected tragic death of pop music icon Michael Jackson at the age of 50. This happening involved a continuous spectacle like no other, exceeding in media saturation the infamous murder trial of celebrity O. J. Simpson in 1995.

If I were to employ a cultural studies framework here, as you suggested, I would depict this multifaceted phenomenon not as a unique and unprecedented event, but as a culturally symptomatic case. The death of Michael Jackson is well suited to a case study undertaken collectively by an undergraduate or graduate class engaged in cultural studies and using ideology and cultural critique. Off the top of my head, I would list as major interlocking domains for inquiry (as potential chapters in a study): family, pop music industry, media, psychology, medicine, law, race, social class, fashion. A book could be composed by the students supported with photographic stills, music clips, and videos stored on an accompanying compact disc.

Among the more arresting facets of the Michael Jackson phenomenon is his postmodern "volatile body": straightened hair; lightened skin; surgically altered face (especially the nose); anorexic body; gender-bending outfits (effeminate gloved hand covered in signature sequins); rumored pedophilic sexuality (despite high-profile heterosexual marriages); and amazingly fluid dancer's bearing on stage and in video (his patented moon walk). What role drugs played in this whole long career remains fuzzy.

The visual features of Michael Jackson's cyborg body seem perfectly matched to our era of spectacle. I would hypothesize that media values very early penetrated Michael Jackson's child star psyche, shaping his self-image and his sense of being looked at 24/7. Being became appearing.

To generalize beyond the Michael Jackson case, celebrity entails the presence not only of permanent publicity, but also of self-surveillance gauged to prevailing norms (conscious and unconscious). Swarms of paparazzi keep watch, forming part of the larger surveillance society. Cameras are everywhere. In addition to surveillance, they prompt exhibitionism while facilitating the rapid spread of information. This is a mixed blessing.

As an aside, a contrast, what could one say in this context about the African American hip-hop nation and rap music? What kind of attention would a death in its higher ranks entail these days or back in its 1990s crossover heydays? I suppose mainstream media would offer less coverage by comparison. Even now thirty plus years after its onset, US black male hip-hop appears too macho, too vulgar, too alienated; it's too "black." Its central icon is the pimp in the post-Civil Rights era role formerly occupied by the outspoken black preacher. The pimp represents black separatism and nationalism. He's a gangster and a threat. In contrast, Michael Jackson, a glamorous Hollywood star, stands for the harmony of ebony and ivory—for non-threatening integration—and savvy business enterprises. He personally purchased the Beatles catalogue of songs for several hundred million dollars. Despite his creative aberrations, mainstream media can embrace that kind of figure. It represents little real threat to white middle- and ruling-class cultures. My point is these images reveal swirls of social values in motion through media. From its outset in the 1970s UK, cultural studies was and remains designed to analyze moral panics, mass-mediated spectacles, and stereotypes. Theory has a role to play.

One other point I would like to stress. I don't take the media's obsession with the death of Michael Jackson as simply distracting from more serious realities such as the US wars in Iraq and Afghanistan, the senate confirmation hearings for the first Latina Supreme Court justice, or the post-election street revolts against the reigning political order in Iran (home of Islamic revolution). Distraction, I reckon, is symptomatic and central to our media-drenched, visually oriented, multichannel, multitrack, multitasking society. I figure the collective MJ case study sketched a moment ago would reveal a considerable amount about contemporary culture—its mechanisms, dispositions, and values (ideology). This would doubtlessly include such things as the relation between entertainment and now permanently embedded media. My point is that the media frenzy over celebrity presents stark evidence about postmodern reality, maybe most notably its intimacy with simulation and with passive viewing that is pleasurable yet repressive. Umberto Eco's idea of the "authentic fake" is perhaps illuminating in the Disney-like theatricalization of Michael Jackson's life and his highly ritualized passing.

DM: Although it would require its own interview, I want to ask you a bit about your work revising the *Norton Anthology* for a second edition. Based on my reading of prior interviews with you and your published thoughts on the first *Norton*, it

seemed to me there were at least three main areas you wanted
to consider in a revision: (1) the possibility of including more
non-Western-oriented theorists; (2) adding theorists born
more recently than 1957, the birthdate of Stuart Moulthrop,
the youngest inclusion in the first edition; and (3) allowing
the *Norton* to move more in the direction of a postmodern
disaggregation by including such things as an electronic
archive that would enable interested readers to, in a sense,
create their own anthology based on materials unavailable
in the limited space of the printed text. Looking backward,
were you able to make headway on any or all of these
tasks? It sounded like the issue of electronic copyrights was
a problem in the first go-round. Did you address that with
Norton in the contract for the revision? Since you did go in
the direction of more non-Western theories, did you need to
enlist a new band of editors to help with the choices? Did you
continue to self-educate on materials you were unfamiliar
with? Given that you selected work from scholars born after
1957, how did you grapple with the issue of their impact on
theory in the long run (if there is such a thing as a long run)?

VBL: The main problem with publishing a printed anthology of
theory selections nowadays that would be richly backed up
by an electronic archive (ideally a complete library) concerns
permissions costs (intellectual property). Currently, fees
range wildly from $10 to $450 per printed page. To reprint
a ten-page article or chapter might cost $4,500. There is no
way to pay for such a vast electronic resource under present
conditions. Note that in the case of the *Norton Anthology
of Theory and Criticism*, we six editors remain committed to
the best contemporary editions and translations, not simply
those out of copyright protection and without fees. We
have expensive versions, for example, of Aristotle's *Poetics*,
Plato's *Republic*, Sidney's *Defence of Poesy*, and quite a few
others, even though cheap and free versions are available. So
maintaining quality over against reducing costs is an issue
too—one that increasingly haunts higher education in our
profit-maximizing era.

On the question of contemporary theorists born in the
post-WW II period, we editors added to the second edition

twenty new figures of whom roughly a dozen are our own contemporaries. Starting from the year of birth 1950, the anthology contains selections from Henry Louis Gates, Eve Kosofsky Sedgwick, Franco Moretti, Dick Hebdige, Steven Knapp and Walter Benn Michaels, bell hooks, Lisa Lowe, Judith Butler, Paul Gilroy, Andrew Ross, Lauren Berlant and Michael Warner, Michael Hardt with Antonio Negri, plus Judith Halberstam. Unlike mathematicians and music composers, academic literary and cultural theorists tend to mature later, generally after 40. These figures have all had an impact on contemporary theory; and we were able to find resonant as well as theoretically rewarding, plus teachable selections from each of them.

We did add four new non-Western theorists, choosing selections from the late twentieth century that fuse peculiarly "foreign" and mainstream concerns. From the Arabic tradition, we have a piece on modernity from the poet Adūnis's *An Introduction to Arab Poetics*. The Chinese tradition is represented by Zehou Li's *Four Essays on Aesthetics: Toward a Global View*, which weaves a hybrid aesthetic theory out of stands from Kant and Marx as well as Chinese traditions. C. D. Narasimhaiah's essay "Towards the Formulation of a Common Poetic for Indian Literatures Today" integrates ideas from T. S. Eliot, F. R. Leavis, and other Westerners with an array of Sanskrit concepts from Medieval times. Kōjin Karatani's opening chapter of *Origins of Modern Japanese Literature* shows how the alien modern Western concept of "literature" traumatically entered the Japanese world of the late nineteenth and early twentieth centuries.

I hasten to add that these four new figures of global theory join several handfuls of others (some carried over from the first edition) who address non-Western topics. I am thinking of Giambattista Vico, Claude Lévi-Strauss, Frantz Fanon, Ngugi wa Thiong'o, Edward Said, Gayatri Spivak, Gilroy, Lowe, and Paula Gunn Allen.

Yes, we did hire consulting editors, specialists, for the Arabic, Chinese, Indian, and Japanese selections. They each presented us with a range of materials to consider that we six editors discussed in detail. The consulting editors went on to draft the headnotes, bibliographies, and annotations that accompany the final selections.

Since I had started thinking in the 1990s about "going global" with theory, I had done preliminary research and reading. The traditions in question go back a thousand or more years so, not surprisingly, there exist massive amounts of materials. This is what led to recruiting consulting editors, experts in the different languages, literatures, and traditions.

DM: I wonder if you could reflect on a few aspects of your own writing style. How do you manage to "sound" so objective and even sincere when rehearsing arguments or complaints about theories or positions that I am sure you hold dear? I am thinking, for example, of parts of the chapter on "Theory Retrospective" concerning cultural studies: "It renounces scholarly objectivity in favor of engaged activism.... It is overly ambitious, even imperialistic, in the range and scope of its objects of inquiry" (*Theory Matters*, 13). Perhaps the point is to show skeptical readers that a cultural theorist CAN be "objective"? You then in the same essay shift gears by turning to writing in the first person, thus owning the "complaints" against cultural studies. "I have my own personal complaints about cultural studies" (13). Can you reflect on this kind of ventriloquism? Would you describe your own critical "voice" as heteroglossic, even as it "sounds" unified?

On the matter of writing style, I consider your "voice" to be unusually humble and at the same time unusually self-confident. By humble I mean that you are willing, as in the example above, to rehearse the arguments of others without feeling that your work is somehow not "original." By confident I mean that you are willing to make large declarations in authoritative tones about your field: "There are five ways to construct histories of contemporary theory" (*Theory Matters*, 35, a sentence selected almost randomly). I am particularly interested in how you gained the confidence to write with such confidence. Like you, I am not from a background that would have predicted that I became an author and an academic. It has been a great struggle for me to overcome my fear that someone who belongs in the club is still looking over my shoulder, waiting to correct mistakes or point out overlooked important information. (Talk about living in a surveillance society!) I bet a lot of graduate students and assistant professors would be interested in how you learned to perform yourself on paper.

VBL: I see myself mainly as a historian of literary and cultural theory. The history of theory, especially in the modern and postmodern periods—those in which I do most of my work—is extremely complex with innumerable voices in contention. Arguments define the field. At any given time numerous schools, movements, and positions coexist in tension. Differences persist not only within and between schools and movements, but also within individual careers and the careers (or phases) of schools. To write a history of contemporary theory and criticism, you absolutely need to ventriloquize many different voices. Not incidentally, I very much like Walter Benjamin's idea of history as an assemblage of quotations. Being able to recount a critical position is what critical understanding amounts to. It's a mode of justice. It produces objectivity effects.

But I think of my way of doing history as being critical, not objective or neutral. It operates on several levels, two of which I'll single out. First, rather than personally enumerating the problems and limitations of a particular movement, figure, or theory, I survey the complaints of other critics, sometimes many other critics. It's a classic review of the research. This provides density as well as nuance and balance. It feels like a trustworthy knowledgeable insider's account. I think of it as communal micro history. Second, I offer first-person assessments from my own standpoint, which I picture to myself as moments of solo work in larger choral ensembles. The effect is of a leading voice separate from others yet in the context of the others. It's thick history with multiple critical edges and tones.

As a historiographer, I have developed some heuristics. I talk about these mainly in my book *Cultural Criticism, Literary Theory, Poststructuralism*. I'll mention a few here, distilling them as imperatives for historians: atomize, totalize, pluralize. In depictions above of contemporary theory, I self-consciously provide a more or less complete list of movements and schools (I totalize). But I also quickly deconstruct these projects into the work of numerous internally different figures (I atomize). Taken far enough, atomization leads to pluralization (poststructuralisms, Marxisms, feminisms). Not surprisingly, I extend this protocol of pluralization to key literary and cultural concepts such as literatures, poetries, and readers. It is often helpful and revealing programmatically, I find, to add an "s." These heuristics play a role in the tone of my work. They assist in establishing a sense of authority, openness, and confidence. And, of course, long hours in archives must also figure somewhere in this account.

Along the way I picked up some specific writing skills that, no doubt, contour my voice and style. From formalism and Geneva phenomenology, I gradually learned to paraphrase respectfully, if not economically and elegantly. Perhaps more pertinent, early in my career I wrote several hundred abstracts for *Abstracts of English Studies* and other publications. If you write enough 150-word summaries of dense 20-page scholarly articles, you come to appreciate not just clarity, but cogency in scholarly writing. You get to the heart of the matter and to aberrations very quickly and economically. What else? I have grown fond, perhaps too fond, of lists and maps, earned generalizations and slogans. They can do good work. Finally, I make it a point—a program, let's say—to end paragraphs with snappy conclusions: what business people and politicians label "take-away points" suited for our too rushed society.

The question of originality has vexed me off and on throughout my career. Here's my main concern. Should a historian aim for originality? I wonder. Did my predecessors, for example René Wellek, seek to be original? One kind of originality comes from the archive. My *American Literary Criticism* is the first panoramic history to include in separate chapters the New York Intellectuals; the existentialists and phenomenologists; the hermeneuticists; and the Black Aesthetics movement. It is a question not merely of (re) discovery, but of breadth of vision. What counts? My concern with internal differences—micro histories—also brings something new to the history of twentieth-century schools and movements of theory that perhaps registers with only a few insiders. Like most historians of my generation, I do history from below and the margins, a new postmodern mode of history of criticism that includes discourses by women, ethnic minorities, "queers," and working classes. This is the work of cultural critique. Lastly, I am a comparatist by instinct. For example, without foregrounding the first-person, I compare and contrast American and Frankfurt School Marxism; Slavic and American formalism; American and Geneva-style phenomenology; Martin Heidegger's and E. D. Hirsch's hermeneutics; European Neo-Marxism and the US New Left; American and German (East as well as West) reception theories; French versus US deconstruction; and American and French feminisms. I remain in the background and render a service. One final thought on originality. Among scholars of literature, graduate students included, histories and anthologies of theory fulfill a service function. These works are not genres where one expects to or readily perceives original treatments. They are "brown cover" texts that you do not acknowledge having read or consulted. It is something of a curse for authors.

DM: I enjoyed your essay on "Blues Southwestern Style" in *Theory Matters*. It is exciting to hear of such a thriving music scene in Oklahoma City. I'm jealous. Nonetheless, I have questions about the essay. Given my current research interests in Jewish cultural studies, I am sensitive to the issue of the relation between such "African American" musical contributions as blues and jazz and their appropriation by "whites." Scholars such as Jeff Melnick in *Right to Sing the Blues* have criticized Jews such as Irving Berlin for benefiting from the commercialization of African American music, and scholars such as Eric Lott and Michael Rogin have focused on the issue of "passing," how Jews in effect enhanced their ambivalent status as "white" by ventriloquizing/masking blackness. Obviously your interest in the blues subculture of Oklahoma City is not motivated by financial profits or passing as white, but still I wondered if you are ever self-conscious about being a well-paid white guy whose subcultural identity revolves around a music that traditionally deals with themes such as poverty and homelessness and social injustice. Maybe in an emotional sense you have experienced many "Stormy Mondays" and sometimes feel that "The Thrill is Gone," but the cause of your distress must be quite different than it was for a B. B. King or a Howlin' Wolf. (Of course, B. B. King is no longer suffering financially, even as he sings about a kind of pain and suffering that he wrote about as a black man coming up in the Jim Crow era.) I realize one does not need to be poor or an African American to suffer. You mention that your daytime identity and job status are checked at the door when you enter the blues scene, implying that the blues subculture thus enables you to participate in a kind of democratic meritocracy in which esteem in the group is based on such things as dedication to the blues and participation in various blues events. You do mention the sharp divide between the African American clubs (which you are able to enter through your friendship with Miss Blues), the main interracial blues scene you inhabit, and the more commercialized blues events that bring in legends such as B. B. King. Do you feel the utopian, non-hierarchical (in terms of day job status) elements of the blues subculture also mask the serious disparities among the participants? Is this a case of a Bakhtinian carnival that turns the tables on power relations for a short time only to enforce the status quo in the end? Does it trouble you that you are in a sense going "under cover" to perform "informal interviews" with various blues people that you then convert into a participant-observer case study that was in part funded by the Oklahoma Humanities Council and the University of Oklahoma and then published in a book—*Theory Matters*—that will allow you, not the others in the blues scene, to accrue cultural capital? Does it matter to you whether or not they know your interest in the blues scene is at least in part a scholarly pursuit?

VBL: I want to start by giving a quick thumbnail sketch of the history of blues music. It matters very much here. And, after all, I am a historical critic and theorist by inclination. The way I conceive it there are five, maybe more, distinct periods or phases. Blues goes postmodern along the way. The first period involves rural acoustic blues from World War I to World War II, followed by a second phase of urban electric music from WW II into the mid-1960s. You can think of these geographically as Chicago preceded by Mississippi Delta blues, both stemming from the African American community. In the third period, young white blues musicians begin to appear during the 1960s and gain prominence. Examples would be the Paul Butterfield Blues Band, Canned Heat, and Johnny Winter, each having a separate regional identity, but a national white audience. A fourth period witnesses the contemporaneous international spread of blues especially to the UK, which begins in the late 1950s and early 1960s. A fifth period commences in the 1970s and 1980s when interracial blues societies and festivals start to appear all across the US and scattered around the globe. As I am having this conversation with you, there are approximately two hundred blues societies, several hundred annual blues festivals, and an extensive infrastructure of blues clubs, record labels, magazines, radio shows, Web sites, etc. And although there exist remnants of the all-black chitlin circuit, the blues scene has been integrated and globalized, postmodernized, for many decades.

White people like me have been devoted to blues music since the 1950s and 1960s. Many leading musicians are white such as Eric Clapton, Bonnie Raitt, and Stevie Ray Vaughan. In all of this, there are elements of emulation and appropriation. But the same dynamic operates for numerous artistic genres. Japanese haiku stems from an ancient alien aristocratic milieu. Yet school children have for decades tried their hand at the form. The same goes for the sonnet, an Italian Renaissance genre soon picked up by English and French poets, but today present on Hallmark cards as well as in creative writing classrooms. It would be a mistake to characterize such transmissions and survivals as thefts, pure and simple. That characterization depends on questionable notions of private property, exclusive ownership, and copyright—all ideas postdating and foreign to haiku, sonnetry and, I would argue, original rural blues.

This question of cultural theft gets us into the history of music copyrighting and recording in the US. Regarding the blues, the main narrative holds that white college students, who in the early 1960s instigated a revival of acoustic blues (cast as folk music), helped elderly black musicians to secure audiences and copyrights. Among older black blues artists today there exists a range of opinions on the issue of appropriation. But not a few seem grateful as well as surprised and proud to have crossed over into the white world and also to have gone global. This transformation has provided much support for blues musicians. Would it have been better or even possible for the blues, including its creation, distribution, and consumption, to remain exclusively within the African American community across the twentieth century? No, I think not.

Blues festivals and shows do approximate carnival. One indicator is that no one asks what you do for a living. I am never asked. And I don't ask. The festivals mix all social classes. But so does walking down a city sidewalk, attending a movie, riding urban mass transit, or dancing in a club. In all this, there is a suggestion, a utopian hint: we can live together.

One of my favorite strands of cultural studies is analysis of subcultures. Undergraduate students enjoy doing research projects in this area. A lot of it entails participant observation and insider accounts. Personally, I've received papers on Goth, emo, rave, hip-hop, fraternity and sorority life, etc. This research talks about such topics as music, dress, body language, sexual conventions, social hierarchies, and cultural politics. Students enjoy writing about what they know while taking distance through critique. But this strand of ethnography, really autoethnography and intimate critique, doesn't approximate going undercover since immersion precedes written formulations. That's how it was for me writing about the blues in a one-off chapter—with no monetary rewards in sight. I got interested in the music many years before I wrote about the blues. My original interest had nothing to do with wanting to publish on the music. As it happened, while I was planning my chapter on the local blues subculture, as an example of cultural studies work, I received a flyer encouraging applications from scholars to the State Humanities Council for $500 research grants. I applied and used the money for travel and materials. I believe local subcultures and cultural scenes are worthy of critical study and support. Certainly, motives for doing so are subject to question.

The subculture research I've seen from undergraduate students tends toward celebration, not critique and not betrayal. This raises questions for class discussion concerning various matters, including the ethics and objectivity of participant observation, plus especially the nature and essential role of critique.

DM: We are arguably in the worst financial crisis since the Great Depression. As a historian of theory, how would you compare and contrast the response of literary critics in the 1930s to that economic meltdown to how you are seeing critics/theorists deal with the financial crisis today? My sense is that there were plenty of "writers on the Left," to borrow a phrase from Daniel Aaron (Steinbeck, Odets, Rukeyser, Hughes), but wasn't literary criticism in the 1930s dominated by formalism? I realize there were left-leaning public intellectuals surrounding the *Partisan Review* as well as figures such as Granville Hicks. You have been calling for a kind of theory that takes economics into account. I think you are not only referring to institutional studies of an imploding academic profession, but also you are encouraging theorists to take on macroeconomic questions such as globalization and the flows of capital. How should a scholar like myself, trained in literary analysis, re-tool for such a daunting task? Math was not my strength even in high school, and I nearly flunked Econ 101 in college.

VBL: I distinguish between political economy and economics. Mainstream academic US economics, a social science, sold its soul to mathematics many decades ago. It got a divorce from political science. Econometrics seeks to be a pure science. It's the leading edge of this autonomous discipline. Economics belongs to the school of business and to laissez-faire finance capitalism in its virulent post-1960s neoliberal form. You cannot find a Marxist or socialist economist in any department of economics, with few exceptions. During the past three decades, Keynesians have gone into the closet. It's part of the retreat of liberalism and the dismantling of the Welfare State, the latter an accomplishment of civilization worth defending. The way I see it politics, psychology, and sociology now have the job of cleaning up the mess created by economics.

I offer fuller critiques of mainstream American economics in my *Postmodernism—Local Effects, Global Flows* and subsequent books. So I won't rehearse that work here. But one place to turn for an alternative is ecological economics.

Concerning the 1930s, Western Marxism of the French, German, and in part Italian traditions made a "cultural turn" in that decade away from Soviet Marxism. With the 1939 pact between the Nazis and Soviets to divide up Europe into separate spheres, US Marxists fled the Communist Party and its Popular Front in droves, turning away from the proletarian revolution along with its aesthetic doctrines. That is what both the Frankfurt school in exile and the post-1937 regrouped *Partisan Review* represent. During the 1960s, many segments of the Western left bid farewell to the working class as the vanguard of revolution. It's the hardhat phenomenon where leading segments of the proletariat turn conservative, nativist, and nationalist. At this time the new social movements became the cutting edge of "transformation" (no longer "revolution"). Here I am thinking of student radicals, civil rights campaigners, women's liberation activists, environmentalists, etc. Jumping ahead, the 1999 protests in Seattle against the non-democratic World Trade Organization symbolize the prominence in the struggle against neoliberal globalization and the New World Order of the expanded new social movements, the "multitude," to use Hardt and Negri's memorable term, a worldwide rainbow coalition, an affective alliance, represented by the World Social Forum built up from micropolitical forms. This is the Popular Front in a viral twenty-first-century form. Other more recent instantiations of the multitude include the Arab Spring, the worldwide Occupy movements, and the antiausterity protests in Greece, Spain, and Portugal. So, while I understand nostalgia for the 1930s, I believe it is going to be only of limited help given our post-industrial, highly financialized, nondemocratic economy. Also it is worth noting that the intelligentsia is now largely inside the university and not outside. Although this embourgeoisement is cooptation, what really matters is the increasing enclosure of everything—including nature, the unconscious, and the imagination—by capitalism. The avant-garde is history. Bohemia is part of the creative class now. Meanwhile, proletarianization and deprofessionalization of the lower tiers of the professions proceed apace. The directors of the global economy—the International Monetary Fund, World Bank, United Nations, World Trade Organization, Group of Eight, World Economic Forum (Davos), plus transnational corporations and non-governmental organizations—all postdate the 1930s.

To repeat an earlier point but now with an added twist, the idea of everyday life, a productive concept for theory and cultural studies, deliberately carries thinking and feeling out of the universities, think tanks, and regulatory agencies into the streets and ordinary homes, especially kitchens. The mission of cultural studies is to rebarbarize theory, bringing it home. If you want to know what's going on in society, check out your own intimate surroundings (financial, emotional, aesthetic) and include family and neighborhoods near and far. At the same time, be wary of the media's purchased and truncated coverage of economics. I don't recommend simply going to the economics department of a US university: the well-being of the populace is not its concern. I advise against moralizing the Great Recession or any other boom-bust crisis. There is rampant greed, yes. But more important is the whole system of regulation. It is an intricately rigged system, thanks in part to the corruption visited upon politics by lobbying and money. It doesn't take an economist to tell you that, for example, the lifting in 1980 of the cap on the maximum interest charged on loans (usury) by Congress would soon create disturbances in the linked realms of money-banking-credit. Floods of credit and debt follow. Banks on every corner. Widespread manipulation of credit standards and ratings. Bankruptcies everywhere. Foreclosures. Vast redistributions and accumulations of wealth. The economics of everyday life, broadly construed, is probably as good a gauge of the real economy as the standard technical indicators.

6

French theory's second life

During the closing decades of the twentieth century, French theory constituted a powerful shaping force on many academic disciplines, especially literary and cultural studies. Now at the opening of the twenty-first century, most of its major figures, born between the two world wars, have passed. Yet a flood of posthumous publications, a second wave, has poured from French presses. As of 2013, there have been, by my rough count, seven posthumous volumes by Jacques Lacan; ten by Roland Barthes (not counting five bulky volumes of the complete works); seven by Louis Althusser; five by Pierre Bourdieu; three by Gilles Deleuze; thirteen by Michel Foucault (not including four big volumes of miscellaneous pieces *Dits et écrits*); and five by Jacques Derrida. More is to come. For example, there are two tomes yet to appear of Foucault's annual courses at the Collège de France (eleven of 13 have thus far been published). Of the projected 43 volumes to be published of Jacques Derrida's annual seminars, only three have seen print. We should expect more posthumous works by Jean Baudrillard, Jean-François Lyotard, and others. The leading French feminists, prolific authors Hélène Cixous, Julia Kristeva, and Luce Irigaray, continue to publish, as do leading male philosophers today, Alain Badiou, Etienne Balibar, Jean-Luc Nancy, and Jacques Rancière. And this group snapshot does not take into account later generations of poststructuralists in France or elsewhere.

The current dominant schools and movements of literary and cultural theory, namely postcolonialism, new historicisms, and cultural studies, do not refute but extend poststructuralist work. What contemporary French theorists took from structuralism and phenomenology—for instance, the focus on social systems and institutions and the attention to temporal sequencing and interactive flows—condition humanistic and social scientific inquiry to this day. French poststructuralist concepts remain essential research instruments such as abjection, biopolitics, cultural capital, deconstruction, docile body, écriture féminine, ideological state apparatus, mirror stage, rhizome, simulation, spectacle, and surveillance society. These key notions continue to shape protocols of close reading, of historicizing, and of critiquing. They fill today's guides, handbooks, and glossaries. French poststructuralist modes of analysis are recognizably different from anything that precedes them (they are distinctive assemblages), and they have not been superseded. In short, they are more durable than anyone living during recent decades in our globalizing consumer societies, so addicted to the newest of the new and to rapid turnovers, had any reason to expect. French theory is not going away anytime soon.

The posthumous publication of Jacques Derrida's seminars promises to be an unparalleled project among the leading first-generation French theorists. It will publish 43 years of seminars and courses (a volume for each year). That covers his teaching in France at the Sorbonne (1960–1964), the École Normale Supérieure in Paris (1964–1984), and the École des Hautes Études en Sciences Sociales (1984–2003) as well as his visiting positions in the US at the Johns Hopkins University (1968–1974), Yale University (1975–1986), the University of California at Irvine (1987–2003), plus in New York from 1992–2003 at the New School for Social Research, the Cardozo Law School, and New York University. The American lectures largely repeated the French, although they were improvised in English after 1987. Galilée is the French publisher (it published more than half of Derrida's many books during his lifetime), and the University of Chicago Press is doing the English translation under the editorship of the British Geoffrey Bennington and the American Peggy Kamuf, longtime Derrida scholars and translators. Derrida always wrote out his material for courses and seminars, which could range anywhere from a few to 15 two-hour sessions. After the 1960s, most of the lectures were taped as well. As I write, three volumes have seen print: *Séminaire La bête et le souverain*, Volume I (2001–2002) and Volume II (2002–2003), published in 2008 and 2010, followed by *Seminaire La peine de mort* Volume I (1999–2000) released in 2012. In 2009, the University of Chicago Press inaugurated its series of English translations when it published Volume I of *The Beast and the Sovereign*. Volume II appeared in 2011. The textual editors of these initial two volumes, Michel Lisse, Marie-Louise Mallet, and Ginettte Michaud, provided the manuscripts with supplementary name indexes, filled in Derrida's documentation, and inserted via footnotes helpful materials from the tapes such as missing words and his improvisations and oral annotations. They set the pattern. The lectures appear to be carefully edited, which augurs well for the scholarly quality of the project. One imminent future for French theory is its well-curated materials from the archives.

In many ways, the often-cited Foucault series of lectures serves as a model, fastidious yet reader-friendly, of posthumous editing and genre packaging of French theory. Each two-hour session is broken into two parts (first and second hours), complete with separate endnotes and explanatory footnotes. And each of these article-length texts is preceded by a short summary of topics (abstract) supplied by editors containing roughly 50–150 words. In addition, there is a meticulous lengthy index of concepts as well as one for names. Each volume ends with an editorial "Situation," an essay covering relevant contexts ranging from Foucault's biography and political milieu to methods and developments across his oeuvre. Where available, Foucault's own retrospective résumé of the course, taken from the *Annuaire du Collège de France*, concludes the dozen or so sessions and precedes the "Situation." Unlike the editors of Derrida's seminars, the Foucault editors work with tapes checked against his notes. So they must systematically add punctuation, paragraphing, and conjectures on missing words; they have to cut repetitions, patch interrupted sentences, and correct grammar. This is in addition to supplying explanatory notes. Accessibility as well as accuracy mark this exemplary work of curating.

By comparison, the Derrida seminars are lightly but no less scrupulously edited. Manuscripts are the source text, with occasional interpolations from tapes signaled by the editors in their footnotes. As was his habit, Derrida often analyzed at length texts and keywords in Greek, German, English, and French, correcting or annotating translations as he proceeded in his close readings. The textual editors document such variants plus improvised additions from the tapes while tracking down references and explaining allusions. Occasionally, they straighten out or let stand oddities with Derrida's use of brackets, parentheses, and quotation marks, which he exploited to the full and not infrequently abused. It is not uncommon for Derrida when quoting a long passage to interrupt it several times with his own long distracting bracketed comments. Unlike the editors of Foucault's courses, the editors of Derrida's seminars do not supply abstracts, résumés, and concluding essays on contexts. There are no concept indexes. The lectures are not divided into two manageable parts. In short, Derrida's seminars are much less reader-friendly than Foucault's. But the same goes for the works he published during his lifetime. To all appearances, his seminars will not be expurgated or "improved." So far so good.

Derrida's first two published seminars, characteristic late works, tend toward rambling meditations, performances of thinking. The nearest recognizable genre is the occasional essay. Introductions and conclusions, more often than not, seem mystifications or provocations, but in any case nothing like abstracts, previews, or summaries. Taken together either packaged as a seminar or each singly, the lectures fall far short of the classical criteria for well-made works. When there is a clear thesis, a rare occurrence, it is continuously modulated and delayed, remaining less than firmly argued from beginning to end. Where French sentence structure can often be more relaxed than English, Derrida's style takes that privilege to extremes. So it is that the promising idea of a clean-cut and comprehensive index of concepts is foreign to Derrida's work. In his case, it's more a matter of invaginated clusters of motifs in motion. The "burial-survivance-fantasm" complex that I discuss in a moment offers a good illustration of Derrida's influential mode of excessive reading. But first I want to consider Derrida's fascinating final observations for his students on reading and textual interpretation, a topic central to *Literary Criticism in the 21st Century*. My prognostication is that Derrida's distinctive mode of deconstructive reading will remain influential for the foreseeable future.

Reading and textual interpretation

At the opening of the ten sessions of *Séminaire La bête et le souverain*, Volume II, Derrida tells his audience, addressing both new members and carryovers from the previous years, he "will do everything so that the seminar just getting underway may be intelligible without the earlier premises and therefore be as independent as possible from the outset and during its development" (36; translations mine). I focus here in Chapter 6 on this free-standing seminar of 2002–2003, Derrida's final course.

What Derrida does in this year's work is compare and contrast two texts, Daniel Defoe's *Robinson Crusoe* and Martin Heidegger's *Die Grundbegriffe der Metaphysik: Welt—Endlichkeit— Einsamkeit* (*The Fundamental Concepts of Metaphysics: World, Finitude, Solitude*). It's less a systematic analysis of the two texts than a characteristic free-form and allusive, meandering discourse on the motifs of human world building and of mortality, especially burial and obsessions surrounding it. Derrida offers innumerable short divagations and takes detours on related major figures, some concentrated, some extended, for instance, Maurice Blanchot, Paul Celan, Sigmund Freud, Immanuel Kant, Jacques Lacan, and a half dozen others, all appearing more or less regularly across his broad oeuvre composed over four decades. Along the way many subsidiary motifs, new and old, often conjoined, are developed and explored for the most part inconclusively yet suggestively. Leading examples here would be mourning, sovereignty, autoimmunity, prayer, as-if trope, animals, *logos*, wheels/circles, nostalgia, and homesickness. At roughly a half-dozen moments, Derrida frets over the loose structure of his seminar, explicitly raising questions about reading and interpretation.

The first instance of Derrida's worrying the cohesiveness as well as cogency of his analysis comes toward the end of the third lecture, following readings of Heidegger and Rousseau but primarily Robinson Crusoe. "Is it artificial and abusive to bring together all these motifs (the mechanical technology of the wheel, self-declared autonomy, self-destructive obsession and autoimmunitary paradoxes that render Robinson Crusoe his own destroyer and Defoe perhaps his own enemy, his own foe, the parrot and the wheel, etc.)?" What to make of this odd and expansive cluster of topics? Derrida's reply "I cannot justify in all rigor, I cannot prove that I am right by another argument but this one, which is to begin with a question or a demand: does it seem to you interesting to listen to what I am saying and thus to read *Robinson Crusoe* otherwise?" (137). Here is a recognizable literary appeal to the nowadays very popular critical criterion of "smartness," meaning surprising and more or less believable quirky innovation in textual interpretation. Today many scholars aim to be smart. It's the kind of reading strategy Derrida carries out perhaps most memorably in linking Hamlet and Marx plus their ghosts across his *Specters of Marx*. In the case of the seminar I would judge this preliminary, highly interesting reading of *Robinson Crusoe* and its cluster of motifs neither artificial nor abusive, but not quite simply believable. Too many questions remain unanswered about authorial intention, the psychology of the protagonist, the dynamics of textual motifs, and the projections of double reading (Heidegger with Defoe). That said, Derridean-styled smart reading here retains its allure and a future.

At one other key moment in the seminar, near the start of the eighth lecture, Derrida offers a page of reflections for his students on textual interpretation. His remarks address three topics, progressing from the necessity of slow linear reading and rereading to factoring in the psychology of each reader like himself to the techniques and benefits of reading two texts in tandem [my brackets].

> [1] It is necessary to read and reread in a linear, continuous, and repeated manner these two works, each of these readings being intended to promise you surprises, changes of emphasis, a thousand discoveries in moments apparently furtive or secondary, etc. .... Years would be necessary for this.... I believe also in the necessity ... and even the fecundity, when I am optimistic and confident, of certain leaps, of certain renewed perspectives for a turning of the text, for a crossing of the route that gives us another view of the ensemble....(289–290)

Then Derrida adds parenthetically in mid-sentence, extending the central motif of routes adapted from Heidegger and Defoe:

> [2] (it goes without saying that each of my choices and perspectives depends here, I will never seek to hide it, largely on my history, my earlier work, my manner of proceeding, directing myself along this route, of my drives, desires, and fantasms, even if I strive always to render them at once intelligible, shareable, convincing, and discussable, open to discussion)....(290)

Here he gives bracketed space to intimate critique, knowing it can be neither denied nor contained. Concerning the texts of Defoe and

Heidegger, he promotes their double complex reading, characterizing both his goals and the parallel motifs of routes in doing so. It's a project of enriching interpretation through multiple perspectives:

[3] To read together the *Seminar* of Heidegger and *Robinson Crusoe*, that is to say, two routes, two discourses [genres] also, on and about routes can multiply the perspectives from which the two vehicles can illuminate with their intersecting brilliance the general cartography and landscape in which we are traveling and driving together, driving one another over all these routes intertwined, interspersed, and overloaded with bridges, fords, one-way and detoured routes, etc. (290)

For students the take-away message comes down to unusually straightforward though arguable advice from Derrida. Read not only repeatedly, carefully, and creatively, but also self-interestedly yet convincingly for your audience. Be on the lookout for odd moments and multiple perspectives. Take chances. Expect telling textual blockages as well as connections. Derrida provides unspoken advice too. Select rich canonical figures and texts on related topics, only ones never before linked. Go for surprise. Don't fret overly about the intentions of the author. Meanwhile, the unconscious of the authors, characters, and readers (yourself included) reveal rich motivations and thematic clusters. Mine them. This is a psychoanalytic version of intimate critique. It's a question of singular personal obsessions, fantasms, and repressions as well as odd displacements, condensations, and symbolizations. The text too has an unconscious. Work on it. Take note interpreters: nothing is necessarily irrelevant in the freighted language of complex textual systems complete with antisystemic elements, particularly contradictions, paradoxes, and dysfunctional sets of binary concepts, all valuable materials for the interpreter.

Derrida is a connoisseur of impasses, double binds, and aporias. As a reader, he goes looking for them; they preoccupy him. A representative instance in the seminar of 2002–2003 occurs with the cluster of three motifs "burial-survivance-fantasm," where he reinscribes keywords and deconstructs traditional binary concepts. This kind of excessive reading has been influential going on five decades now. And, I predict, it has a future.

Life death theme

The texts of Defoe and Heidegger address a range of common topics: the state of nature, solitude, the world and its configuration, human sovereignty over animals, gods and prayer (*logos*), technology (for example, the wheel), homesickness, plus life, death, and modes of burial. What sets Derrida to work are Heidegger's statements that animals are poor in world, and that they do not relate to the entirety of being. Moreover, they do not die, but rather perish or finish living. In addition, tradition tells us they do not speak, pray, lie, or laugh. They are neither nostalgic nor melancholic. They lack history. They are incapable of the uniquely human "as if" and "as such" transcendental modes of rationality. According to Derrida, all this animal lore is well known and a banal part of traditional thought. He excoriates the self-interested, solipsistic generalization of all animals to the one category "animal" (280). He labels primitive the idea that the animal doesn't have language (310). To generalize, he is critical of Defoe's and Heidegger's handling of animals and, by implication, of their unreflective dominating sovereign standpoints characteristic of Western philosophical thought. Parenthetically, this is ideology critique yet without the word "ideology" mentioned anywhere in the seminar or, as far as I know, in Derrida's oeuvre. His celebrated deconstructions of several dozen fundamental Western binary concepts instantiate cultural critique à la Derrida.

It is said that animals don't die, and that they don't have burial rituals. But humans do, which defines their mortality. Derrida explores this line of thought, particularly the simple binary opposition between life and death. Yet he does so in a scattered somewhat distracted manner across the seminar, which, nevertheless, generates some striking leaps of thought on fantasms and some rewarding shifts of perspectives on "survivance" (life death).

Much discussion occurs in the seminar about fantasms of the "living dead," of "dying alive," of being "buried alive," and of being "swallowed alive." Robinson Crusoe, for instance, is terrified and obsessed by thoughts of an animal or cannibal who might swallow him alive as well as by storms at sea and earthquakes that would do the same. As much literature testifies, it is possible for some other to burn me, eat me, swallow me, or bury me while I am alive. People and cultures plan their burial rights focused usually on how to settle cadavers, a decision generally overseen by the family, community, and state. In any event, stresses Derrida, the line between life and death is regularly crossed, consciously and unconsciously, in imagining death, worrying it, planning for it, and regulating it. It's a matter of fantasms, to use Derrida's frequent psychoanalytical terminology in the final seminar and elsewhere:

> It goes without saying that the decision on this subject (burial rather than cremation) can only be the decision of a living not a dead person (what would be the decision of a dead person? Isn't it impossible? Doesn't the concept of decision imply at least life and the living person disposing of a future? ...); we need to consider this decision from the point of view of the survivors, the heirs, or the one who gives the instructions about the moment when he or she is going to die but is not yet departed, and can thus speculate on his or her own death only through the imagination or the fantasm of the living dead, at the limit of the dead one who lives enough to see him or her self die and be buried ....(212–213)

The mixed undecidable state of the living dead Derrida labels *survivance*. "Like respiration itself, nothing is for me as natural, spontaneous, habitual, unthought-of, automatic, and indispensable to life as to be obsessed by the *post mortem*, fascinated, worried, and constrained ... " (249). The idea of death infiltrates and shapes life. It's a mode of haunting that produces specters in our dreams, arts, and philosophies. The line between thinking and imagining, thought and imagination, implodes, notably on the subject of death, yours and mine. Living summons survivance.[1] The future invades and haunts the present.

Derrida provocatively extends the deconstructive concept of survivance to the life death of the book, to archives, and to reading

---

[1]The word "survivance" has been around for centuries in French and English. Derrida's various deconstructions and reinscriptions of the life/death binary opposition appear across his vast oeuvre from the 1970s on. Gerald Vizenor (Ojibwa) famously inflects this poststructuralist term from a Native American perspective.

cast as resuscitation, which activity also touches on the community. "A book, the survivance of a book, from the first moment, is a living dead machine, surviving, the body of a thing buried in a library, bookstore, in some caves, urns, drowned in the worldwide waves of the Web, etc., but a dead thing which resuscitates each time the breathe from a living reading, each time that the breathe of the other or the other breathes ... " (194). Derrida propounds an interactive view of life and death that neither Defoe nor Heidegger could consciously subscribe to. He assigns a profound role to the other against the notion of pure solitude of the existential or desert island sort. This encompasses both the external other and the other in me. Community appears in the background, yet it is there borne along in language as well as social convention.

There is more to survivance, fictional and real. It's an odd kind of sovereign non-sovereign force or power in Derrida's account:

> Since one cannot be at once dead and living, the dying living person may be only a fantasmatic virtuality, a fiction, if you wish, but this fictive or fantasmatic virtuality diminishes by nothing the real omnipotence of what shows itself in the fantasm, omnipotence that no longer leaves, never departs, and organizes and commands the whole of what one calls life and death, life death. This force of omnipotence belongs to a beyond of the opposition between being and not being, life and death, reality and fiction or fantasmatic virtuality. (192–193)

For Derrida, death is almighty in its reach, and no god will save us. Survivance is what we have in place of heaven-purgatory-hell. Others insure and protect afterlife such as it is, stemming from imagination, thinking, fear of desecration, conventional burial rites, and the sense of responsibility. It's a matter here of an atomized sovereign force manifested in imagination, fantasm, and *logos* (the latter defined as discourse, rationality, and convention). But just here Derrida's claims for the omnipresence of fantasm strike me personally as unconvincing, hyperbolic, and transcendentalist yet, for all that, still provocative.

Jacques Derrida spent a lifetime at the crossroads of literature and philosophy. He was a historian of philosophy, but philosophy was never enough. Literature regularly supplemented philosophy, sometimes enriching, sometimes usurping it. Here is a final exemplary passage, difficult and wily, that aims to tie up, to thematize, the loose threads of the 2002–2003 seminar:

> There is not any logic or *logos* of the fantasm or of the fantom or the spectral. Unless the *logos* itself may be precisely *the* fantasm, the element itself, the very origin and resource of the fantasm, the form and formation of fantasm, and even of the revenant.
>
> That is why on all the topics we treat here, sovereignty, animal, living dead, buried alive, etc., the spectral and the posthumous, and indeed, the dream, the oneiric, fiction, so-called literary fiction, the so-called literature of the fantastic will still be less inappropriate, more pertinent, if you prefer, than the authority of watchfulness, than the vigilance of the ego, and than the consciousness of so-called philosophical discourse. (262–263)

It is literature, not philosophy, that gives us to think the living dead, the fantasm, and survivance. Like dreams, it plumbs the unconscious; it goes beyond conscious attention and philosophical reason. The *logos* criticized in Derrida's early work, notably in the famous critique of traditional Western logocentrism in his *Of Grammatology*, is not the enriched *logos* of this late work. The latter is something else. Fantasm flows in the place of pure reason, logic, and neat binary oppositions, three stocks in trade of philosophy and logocentrism. The springs of the unconscious infiltrate involuntarily the ego, bringing to bear dreams, revenants, and fantasms, the stuff of literature. Death does not simply come at the end of the road marked by burial rituals. It is there from the start, a fantasm shaping life. Derrida here provides a most memorable example of the widespread postmodern return of the Gothic specter. Just so, the 43 volumes of his annual seminars will come back to life.

Critical judgment

The last seminar of Derrida, consisting of ten lectures delivered in 2002–2003, put in the form of a 400-page published book, has strengths and weaknesses warranting critical assessment. Like much of his work, particularly the late works, it is loose in structure and style. From a scholarly point of view, it is quirky, inventive, daring—in a word—inimitable as well as excessive. On its chosen topics it offers rewards along the way, but no doubt too few and far between for most contemporary fast readers, me included. It feels slow and meandering. One quickly learns to look for the nodal points, the golden passages where connections at last occur, patterns emerge, and insights crystallize. They are scattered across the work, as are moments of incoherence and deadends. Reading Derrida in seminar becomes a workout as well as a treasure hunt, as is often the case with his other texts.

Derrida breezes past contemporary postcolonial, feminist, and Marxist readings of *Robinson Crusoe*, offering perfunctory nods. That is too bad, although it is perhaps an understandable judgment call. A professor can't cover everything in one seminar. Still, to jettison such cultural critiques seems malpractice at this point in academic history. Also he spends too much time on Heidegger, speaking comparatively. He is particularly preoccupied with Heidegger's use of *Walten/walten* (German noun/verb designating govern, rule, reign). He notes that Heidegger surprisingly does not employ the concept of sovereignty, which was very much in the air during the interwar period. What takes its place, Derrida belatedly discovers after a lifetime of reading Heidegger, is evidently *Walten/walten*, an undecidable pre-metaphysical concept connecting life and death via its primordial force, violence, and absolute power that mysteriously flows through Nature, politics, theology, philosophy, and law like an originary drive and ultra-sovereign form of sovereignty. But Derrida remains mystified and unconvincing, coming to no satisfying or sure position, not to mention any judgment. This was evidently unfinished business to be taken up later. Other shortcomings of this seminar? When all is said and done, there is not much offered on animals beyond rehearsing Defoe's and Heidegger's views (compare Derrida and Roudinesco). Ironically, the animal serves as a foil for human being once again. It is also ironic that the title figures, beast and sovereign, receive scant attention in the end.

To conclude this assessment of the book, let me return to the plan for the autonomy of the seminar. The major focus, if there is *one*, of Derrida's final course falls on human life and death as portrayed in *Robinson Crusoe* and *The Fundamental Concepts of Metaphysics*, accompanied by occasional comparisons with a dozen or so major figures. The most productive figures for Derrida and the audience turn out to be arguably Blanchot, Freud, and Kant. The least rewarding are, again arguably, Genet, Hegel, and Levinas, who in any case receive only passing commentary in a few pages. But Derrida refers frequently in footnotes to his earlier works on many of these figures. Indeed, this seminar is deeply rooted in Derrida's sprawling corpus as well as the tradition of Western philosophy and the Great Books. So his plan to make this course free-standing, however understandable, goes amiss. Without their intertextual backgrounds, often thick and intricate, Derrida's lectures can appear willfully allusive, unmotivated, and unrigorous. Too many routes get provocatively opened but not followed to any ends. It's impossible to bracket context and intertext in the interests of purified free-standing close reading.

Futures for French theory

Like Foucault's courses at the Collège de France, Derrida's lectures during the latter part of his career were public events with packed houses and heterogeneous audiences. This raises interesting questions and prospects. To whom did the philosopher intend to speak in this situation with tapes and cameras rolling? Looking to the future, it is likely such performances will be put posthumously on CDs, DVDs, and online archives. What will be the future, the afterlife, of the intellectual property of contemporary celebrity public intellectuals? In the short and long runs, it will be a question of survivance not only for the legal estates, but also for the public domain as well as for intellectuals and scholars. It's a matter, in large part and at present, of digital files and multimedia platforms. But for tomorrow, who knows?

Might the 43 seminars of Jacques Derrida receive second life not only as books but as searchable electronic files or, again, as CDs or DVDs or online video casts? The maverick mid-career French philosopher Michel Onfray (b. 1959, two generations younger than his admired poststructuralists), author of 60 books, has made his lectures on the history of philosophy available in 14 packs of 12 CDs each (published 2004–2010). At midpoint in the series, the last two discs of each pack record question-and-answer sessions with the audience. It is worth mentioning that a three DVD set exists of Gilles Deleuze's *Abecedaire* (eight hours of television interviews), as do roughly a dozen audio CDs of his courses on Spinoza, Leibniz, and cinema, plus an immense online compendium of his seminar transcripts on webdeleuze. Jacques Lacan's legendary 1973 television lecture *Psychoanalysis* is available in French on video as well as in book form. The famous Foucault versus Chomsky debate exists on video and in print. Moreover, issued by Des Femmes Press, a five-CD package (or alternatively a four-cassette pack) of Derrida reading *Circonfession*, taped in 1993, set to music in 2006, followed this publisher's earlier issue of his *Feu la cendre* in its series Library of Voices. Beyond these copyrighted items, there exist innumerable bootleg tapes of Derrida making presentations. There are many unpublished recordings of French theorists, both audio and video, in the archives of the RTF (French Radio and Television Broadcasting) and the INA (National Audiovisual Institute), not to mention Bernard Pivot's TV interview show, *Apostrophes*. One can foresee innumerable permutations in formats and in packaging. With Derrida one can imagine, for instance, the top ten lectures about literature on CDs; or Derrida's lectures on psychoanalysis available in DVD format; or his scattered late lectures on politics, ethics, and law edited and videocast online; or his exemplary deconstructions of key Western binary concepts like life and death anthologized electronically and suitable for e-readers. My concluding point is that there are futures for French theory, some predictable, others unforeseeable. On this news, antitheorists may read and weep.

7

Second lives of Jacques Derrida

More books and articles have been published by and about Jacques Derrida than any other contemporary philosopher. It's a veritable scholarly industry that has been thriving for five decades, with more to come. Following its first phase, the second archival stage of the French theory renaissance promises decades of future scholarship. The excess of Derrida's own scholarship matches the excesses of his philosophy and writing. By the time he died at the age of seventy-four in 2004, Derrida had published seventy books, many hundreds of articles, and given an extraordinary number of interviews and guest lectures in fifty countries. He was the world's most prominent and most traveled philosopher. Yet little is known about his life. Instead the substance and the style of his deconstructive philosophy have attracted all the attention.

But with Benoît Peeters's *Derrida* (2010; trans. 2012), we have an extensively researched full-length biography packed with information. The publication of biographies, autobiographies, and memoirs of contemporary theorists, so many since the early 1990s, is a distinctive postmodern phenomenon (Franklin). It is connected with the rise of the public intellectual dating from the 1980s as well as with the voracious appetite of the 24/7 media, book publishers included, for real-life material. The second lives of French theorists such as Foucault, Barthes, and Derrida typically reveal scandalous facts, giving added meaning to the term "second lives." The ongoing implosion of public and private spheres, characteristic of postmodernity, opens private life to ever-expanding exposure. Almost nothing appears private any longer. Social media vastly facilitates exposure. The Derrida biography bears witness to these phenomena. From the perspective of antitheorists who advocate criticism and theory focused resolutely on self-effacing close reading of canonical texts, the recent elevation of leading literary and cultural intellectuals to celebrity status, complete with biographies, autobiographies, and especially memoirs, attests to the corruption of the humanities, not to mention the university and society. Yet the humanization of famous academic figures has a whipsaw effect: it raises lives up and whittles them down. This is the case with the Derrida biography where he is treated as a flawed human being as well as an academic star.

It turns out Derrida was a workaholic, a hoarder, and a seducer. The theme of the life appears to be *de trop*, in a word, excess. But the biographer tries to avoid any grand thesis, staying close to the facts and remaining impartial. Published in Flammarion's long-running French series Grandes Biographies, this life story has notable strengths and peculiar weaknesses. Though a mixed success, it makes a valuable contribution to scholarship. We should expect more life writings on French and other theorists.

In place of a master theme or claim about Derrida, the Peeters's biography offers innumerable petits récits. A sequence of roughly four-page bits takes the overall form of a muted picaresque adventure set atop a chronicle. Summaries of Derrida's works do not appear; his accomplishments are assumed. Discussions of his publications focus on the editors and publishers involved plus, where of interest, popular and scholarly receptions. This work is neither an intellectual history, nor a hagiography, nor an exemplary life. Instead it combines biography of Derrida's personal life, professional career, and institutional history. It provides numerous glimpses inside the world of academic theory. The working premise is clear: this subject is a famous person. Much telling information is imparted and secrets are revealed.

The biography orchestrates a veritable flood of information utilizing a three-part structure: (I) Jackie (1930–1962), (II) Derrida (1963–1983), and (III) Jacques Derrida (1984–2004). The initial break, 1962, is the year Derrida published his first book and changed his first name. Also that year his family fled the Algerian revolution and moved from Algiers to Nice. Derrida was a postcolonial subject living in diaspora. The roots of the family in Algeria stretch back five centuries, pre-dating the French colonization of the 1830s. The second break, 1983, marks a handful of significant events. After twenty years of teaching at Paris's celebrated École Normale Supérieure (ENS), Derrida left it for the nearby École des Hautes Etudes en Sciences Sociales, where he would teach for the next twenty years. The still thriving antiestablishment Collège International de Philosophie (CIPh) was planned and headquartered in Paris with Derrida as its cofounder and first director. His close friend, colleague, and fellow deconstructor the Belgian American Paul de Man died from cancer in 1983. Around the same time Derrida had also become a major public figure following his arrest, detention, and release in Soviet Prague on trumped-up charges of drug possession. The highest levels of the French government as well as the media got involved. Derrida's image was splashed all over newspapers, magazines, and television. Before then, although it is hard to believe, he refused to be photographed. From that moment, he was a celebrity.

Based on the biographical revelations, Derrida was a democratic socialist quietly critical of Soviet and Chinese totalitarianisms and sympathetic to the Algerian drive for independence. Yet he maintained discrete silence on much of contemporary politics until the 1990s when he emerged as an unambiguous critic of post-Cold War triumphant free-market capitalism and American-style imperialism. Given that his main tutelary figure, early and late, was Heidegger, infamous for his resolute silence on his Nazi past, Derrida's politics were long suspect and justifiably so. But the shocking 1987 *New York Times* revelation of Paul de Man's youthful anti-Semitic journalistic writings during World War II put deconstruction and Derrida's political sympathies on the public agenda. Behind all these political events lay some long-buried childhood experiences that Derrida, a Sephardic Jew, endured in Algeria. At the age of twelve he was summarily dismissed from school for being a Jew thanks to an anti-Semitic decree of the Vichy government. It was a moment of personal trauma as well as stigma and shame. His family enrolled him in an alternative Jewish school where he was extremely unhappy. According to his own testimony, afterwards he remained forever wary of any and all enforced community, dogma, and authority. This accounts, I believe, for an antinomian if not libertarian streak running through his politics as well as his philosophy.

There is a great deal of additional telling detail in the biography concerning Derrida's politics. It sheds new light on French poststructuralist circles. For instance, his early 1970s split from the journal *Tel Quel* and its notable editors Philippe Sollers and Julia Kristeva resulted largely from their turn to Maoism at the time of the Chinese Cultural Revolution. Derrida's leadership role in the Groupe de Recherches sur l'Enseignement Philosophique, especially active in the 1970s, stemmed from his criticism of certain right-wing national educational policies of President Valéry Giscard d'Estaing. His co-organizing and directing during the early 1980s of the CIPh came about through the encouragement of newly elected Socialist Party President François Mitterrand's government. It was this government that facilitated Derrida's release from jail in Prague. The short lecturing visit to Prague, sponsored by the international Jan-Hus Educational Foundation established in 1980 at the University of Oxford, shared in the organization's broad anti-Soviet campaign to support *samizdat* and to fight censorship in teaching and publication. One of the more telling revelations here concerning Derrida's politics is an unpublished private nineteen-page single-spaced letter of April 27, 1961 that he sent to historian Pierre Nora, author of *Les Français d'Algérie* (1961). Derrida argues as a self-conscious French Algerian against many of Nora's generalizations and for a future postcolonial multicultural society in Algeria. This carefully articulated position-taking remained private, and Derrida did not speak out on Algeria until subsequent troubles occurred in the 1990s. This information gives credence to the contentious idea of a late versus an early Derrida. It's worth noting, though the biographer misses this point, that Derrida was one of the few prominent French male theorists of his cohort publicly to support at various moments feminism, anti-racism, immigrant rights, and other new social movements.

The author bypasses the Anglo-sphere cultural wars of the 1980s, the time of the Thatcher–Reagan regimes and the vociferous conservative condemnations of French theory and deconstruction, which in 1987 had fastened on the de Man affair. Such attacks pressured Derrida to go public and to do so in major media. Not incidentally, this is the moment when the mainstream media were increasingly adopting tabloid-style sensationalism in the context of both the speeded-up news cycle and the proliferation of outlets. The fin-de-siècle transformation of leading academic scholars and theorists like Derrida into public intellectuals and celebrities was often initially a matter of fighting back.

Derrida's long relationship with French educational institutions remained vexed throughout his life. The biography provides poignant cases beyond the early expulsion and the subsequent uneven school attendance during adolescence. After he left Algeria for the first time at age nineteen and entered Paris's Louis-le-Grand Lycée in preparation for ENS entrance examinations, Derrida failed twice and ended up spending three years at this famous preparatory institution before finally succeeding. The biographer opines it was and would remain a matter of idiosyncratic creativity versus institutional discipline: Derrida was not fitted by temperament to jump through bureaucratic educational hoops even though he publicly bowed to their necessity. Ironically, his job at ENS as middling "caïman," along with fellow French Algerian caïman and lifelong close friend Louis Althusser, entailed preparing students for the rigorously prescribed written and oral agrégation examinations. The biography plays down tensions between Derrida, a non-Communist, and dedicated Communist Party member, Althusser, emphasizing instead their long-term personal closeness. It's a different story, yet only hinted at, with the academic adherents of the two philosophers. Opposing camps came into being at the ENS and elsewhere, including the US and the UK, where it often came down to a yes or no for Marxism, which remains to this day a fault-line among theorists and critics.

Other telling vexations with the French educational establishment occurred later. When Derrida was nominated in 1980, for example, to replace retiring Paul Ricoeur at Nanterre University, he went through a rigorous process before being turned down. Initially he said no, but Ricoeur, earlier his boss at the Sorbonne, persuaded him. This candidacy prompted Derrida to submit and successfully defend works before a distinguished jury of philosophers and a large public in order belatedly, embarrassingly so, to complete the required doctoral thèse d'État. The sole remaining hurdle was an interview with the national Conseil Supérieur des Corps Universitaires where several members read aloud—sarcastically—passages from the work. By then Derrida had published ten books. Only one person voted for him. The position went to Georges Labica, a comparative unknown. Derrida was humiliated and incensed. But the final straw came a decade later: it was the failure of friend Pierre Bourdieu and ally Yves Bonnefoy, both at the Collège de France, to get Derrida elected to this most distinguished institution where

Claude Lévi-Strauss, Michel Foucault, and Roland Barthes had very recently held posts. The author quotes from his interview with philosopher Dominique Lecourt concerning Derrida as a rising academostar in France: "Many colleagues detested him at the time, for his brilliance, his foreignness, and his total lack of concessions" (401–402; translations mine).

Derrida had much better luck with universities abroad. Despite its dubious status at home, French theory started going global by the early 1970s. Beginning in 1968, Derrida taught compact annual seminars lasting three to four weeks. He commenced this mission at the Johns Hopkins University, then Yale University, followed by the University of California at Irvine. In the earliest years, when he suffered from fear of flying, American students came to Paris, where Derrida offered short supplementary study abroad seminars arranged by Hopkins, Yale, and Cornell. It was during the 1980s that he began to travel copiously, delivering lectures across the world, becoming a veritable globetrotting emissary of theory. From 1992 to 2003 Derrida, by now a recognizable worldwide celebrity, lectured regularly in New York City at the New School for Social Research, the Cardozo Law School, and New York University. Not insignificantly, he switched to lecturing in English in the late 1980s, expanding his outreach far beyond followers and restricted audiences.

Still, all was not smooth sailing at foreign universities, as several nasty cases illustrate. In addition to the de Man affair, there was one especially high-profile international campaign undertaken during May 1992, most notably by philosophers, against Derrida receiving an honorary doctorate from the University of Cambridge. The biography quotes both an article in *Der Spiegel* referring to Derrida's ideas as "a poison for young people" and a famous letter accompanied by twenty-two signatures in the London *Times* that cast Derrida as a nihilist and Dadaist. From the late 1970s onwards Derrida was a lightening rod among humanities scholars. When the Cambridge faculty put it to a vote in mid-May, Derrida's award garnered 336 for and 204 against. This is considerable opposition, embarrassingly so, for an honorary degree. Later there was an incident in 2004 at UC Irvine concerning Derrida's archives. During the early 1990s he had deposited a treasure trove there with the library's special theory collections, but he angrily decided against augmenting it, leaving a lacuna from 1996 to 2004. This affair spilled over into an ugly posthumous lawsuit of UCI against the Derrida family, which the university withdrew in 2007. As the biographer has good reason to know, the lacuna was then corrected with substantial Derrida archives at L'Institut Mémoires de l'Édition Contemporaine near Caen, where many related collections are housed, for example, those of Althusser, CIPh, Foucault, and *Tel Quel*. Under duress and in the end, Derrida came "home" in extremely tense and embattled circumstances. And it was a case of scholarly archives.

The consequences of major and minor philosophical disputes, followed often by belated rapprochements—for example, with Foucault, Bourdieu, and Jürgen Habermas—which are scattered across his life, reveal Derrida's expanding professional networks as well as flashpoints in the theory world. In this regard, Peeters's biography intermittently frames stories of academe as an elitist subculture from his own populist middlebrow perspective. Younger by five years, Derrida was a student of Foucault's at the ENS. His first academic lecture in Paris—delivered at the Sorbonne—was a pointed deconstructive assessment in 1962 of Foucault's *Folie et déraison: Histoire de la folie à l'âge classique* (1961). Foucault was in the audience. He found the lecture insightful and in several cited letters congratulated Derrida, encouraging him to get it published. Five years later they quarreled as editorial board members of the leading journal *Critique* about a paragraph in a review essay that in passing praised Derrida's initial criticism of Foucault. Five years after that, Foucault wrote a critical response to its reprinting in a Japanese revue. That same year, 1972, Foucault also wrote an infamous tough and belittling second response to Derrida as an appendix to the reprinting of *Histoire de la folie*. He sent an inscribed copy to Derrida. Following that moment, the two philosophers did not converse for a decade. But upon Derrida's arrest in Prague, Foucault spoke out forcefully on his behalf. And shortly thereafter, Foucault invited Jacques and his wife Marguerite Derrida to his residence for a party greeting a visiting American professor. In the end, there was rapprochement between the two philosophers, but not their many followers.

For Anglo-American followers of French theory, the fallout of the Derrida–Foucault quarrel prompted lasting division. From the 1980s onwards, Foucaultians and Derrideans cast one another as opponents. The biographer characteristically does not spend any time on the theoretical stakes of the dispute. But combatants remember it today both in the contending crude shorthand formulations of "discourse" versus "textuality" as well as cultural critique versus deconstructive close reading and in the stark battle lines drawn between celebrated followers Edward Said and Paul de Man plus their students.

Derrida's relationship with Bourdieu was similarly tumultuous. They started out as friends, but quarreled, finally renewing their friendship later in life. Born the same year and neither one from the Parisian bourgeoisie, they were students together at Louis-le-Grand and ENS. Moreover, they fulfilled their military service in Algeria in the same area and dined weekly there. The biographer does his homework and provides a great deal of detail about Derrida's early years. Just after military service, Bourdieu turned away from philosophy to embrace anthropology, and then he turned again only this time to sociology, a low status discipline in France at that moment. In championing sociology, Bourdieu increasingly attacked philosophy, especially Heideggerian strands. During the 1970s he criticized Derridean philosophy in his book on Heidegger and also notably in the closing pages of the most famous of his several dozen books La Distinction (1979). Animosity particularly flared up during spring 1988, visible in the pages of Libération, when the newspaper ran an interview with Bourdieu on Heideggerianism, followed a week later by a stinging response from Derrida. The biography convincingly casts as the stakes of this debate not only intragenerational rivalry and preeminence, but also the hierarchy of French disciplines. Insofar as philosophy arrogantly presented itself as the queen of the disciplines and arbiter of acceptable and effective argumentation, it drew fire, especially from social scientists like Bourdieu or, for that matter, Foucault. Eventually, though, Bourdieu and Derrida came to join forces from the 1990s onwards for a range of causes such as establishing the Parlement International des Écrivains, the campaign for Derrida's election to the Collège de France, and the struggle against triumphant Anglo-Saxon neoliberalism in support of the increasingly embattled Welfare State, a widely shared ongoing common cause among theorists in European and Anglophone countries.

As Anglophone cultural studies and new historicisms came to prominence in the 1980s and 1990s—an institutional turn of events the Derrida biographer overlooks—sociology became a central discipline, ensuring a place of eminence for Bourdieu's groundbreaking sociology of culture. Meanwhile Derrida's influence during this period was itself very broadly disseminated beyond Yale deconstruction (in disarray since the de Man scandal), most notably to feminism, postcolonial studies, and queer theory. But to this day, deconstruction and cultural studies along with new historicisms remain suspicious of one another. These transformations foreshadow and parallel the disorganization of the field of theory and criticism in the fin de siècle, a phenomenon outside the tightly circumscribed scope of the biography, yet in full flower today.

With challenges to his work mounting, Derrida operated more and more on a friend/enemy basis adjudicated quickly. His adherents often followed suit. He sometimes acted in a paranoid as well as hasty manner. Supporters, friends, and family confirm this pattern. For instance, he distanced himself from Gayatri Chakravorty Spivak, pioneering translator of his work, early supporter, and student of de Man's, because in Derrida's view she did not sufficiently support de Man at the time of the scandal. He fell out with Harold Bloom at the same time. There are many other examples of famous intellectuals and institutions put summarily on Derrida's enemies list. The biographer believes this dynamic was the flip side of Derrida's all-encompassing fidelity as friend. But here he tries too hard to balance the scales, a temptation he often finds difficult to resist. A better explanation has to do with the frantic pace of media debates during the culture wars, a time not conducive to slow deliberation, civility, or painstaking scholarly dialogue.

The biography makes public many personal matters, for example, concerning Derrida's health. In this it has a tell-all quality. During adulthood Derrida's physical health was good, despite persistent bouts of melancholy sometimes slipping into depression, plus a tendency to hypochondria and fear of dying. As a student at Louis-le-Grand and ENS, he suffered serious bouts of test anxiety and insomnia, perhaps contemplating suicide. He used sleeping and pep pills to get by. In these years he survived on a special diet. For five years early in his career, he could not endure air travel. But the one thing that stands out across his 50 years in the academy is nonstop personal complaining about overwork, burnout, and lack of time for reading and writing. Derrida was evidently an obsessive-compulsive workaholic, we are left to conclude. While the author states in his brief introduction that Derrida was a "fragile and tormented man," the biography does not bear out the claim. At most there were moments, apparently justified, of complaint, but his voluminous work and travel seem clearly to override fragility. It is characteristic of leading intellectuals today to be productive in seemingly superhuman ways. Derrida leads the pack in this regard.

Although Peeters's account is resolutely not a psychobiography, it does provide considerable background on Derrida's family, close relationships, and personality, yet without elaboration or assessment. Derrida's father, a traveling beverage salesman, worked hard for very little. As a teenager, Derrida came to sympathize with his limited success. It turns out it was his father who arranged a two-year teaching position for Jackie at a school for the children of French military personnel in Algeria following ENS completion and a year abroad in the United States. At the time, Derrida was military personnel (non-uniformed at his request) stationed at the edges of the Algerian War. Very little is said about his mother, a traditional housewife, although Derrida's finest autobiographical writing, *Circonfession* (1991), records with pathos her final two years and demise in that year from Alzheimer's disease following a stroke. Nothing much is offered on Derrida's older brother and younger sister, though both were interviewed. However, the memory of the early death of his younger brother, Norbert (1938–1940), remained with him. The brother's picture along with his father's held a prominent place on Derrida's work desk. It appears to be a case of lifelong mourning, a theme he would later often revisit. Since he vacationed every summer with his extended family throughout his life, we are left to infer that family was very important to Derrida, though he himself did not address it head-on in his writings.

Of Derrida's wife and children we get truncated sketches. Born two years after Jacques, future wife Marguerite Aucouturier, a Catholic with maternal family in Czechoslovakia, met Derrida while he was at ENS. They spent the academic year 1956–1957 on an exchange appointment at Harvard University. Fearing separation once military service in Algeria began in the autumn, they married in June 1957 in Massachusetts. It appears neither one held the institutional rituals of marriage in high regard. She earned money as a translator from Russian and English and from the mid-1970s as a child psychoanalyst, an admirer as well as translator of Melanie Klein. The biographer is uncharacteristically vague here, doubtlessly because he needed Marguerite Derrida's cooperation and, based on the acknowledgments, he received it in the form of multiple interviews with her and access to archives and to others. That being the case, Benoît Peeters's book should be regarded as an authorized biography written amidst the crosscurrents of Derrida's friends, family, and followers with occasional brief nods to his enemies. The wide world of theory is ever-present yet on the outer fringes of the spotlight.

Concerning the rest of the immediate family, the sons Pierre and Jean Derrida, born several years apart in the mid-1960s, both went on to complete philosophical studies at the ENS and both published first books: Pierre Alféri, *Guillaume d'Ockham, le singulier* (1989) and Jean Derrida, *La Naissance du corps (Plotin, Protius, Damascius)* (2010). The older son, now a writer, changed his name not wanting to compete with his father, who we learn was initially unhappy about the change. As he goes along, the biographer indicates that Marguerite Derrida stuck by her man through thick and thin, assuming traditional wifely duties, even when Jacques strayed.

Derrida had a twelve-year relationship with philosopher Sylviana Agacinski, a generation younger (born 1945). She gave birth to their child Daniel in 1984, the year the relationship ended. A few years later Agacinski joined and then married Lionel Jospin, who raised Daniel. When Jospin ran for President in 2001–2002, the French media publicized the Derrida–Agacinski affair to Derrida's utter dismay. He tried to keep it a secret and would not discuss it with anyone. As one of his book titles reveals, Derrida had a taste for the secret, which he considered a key feature of democracy against the omniscience sought by totalitarianisms as well as media and national security states. The biographer guesses Derrida sent Agacinski a thousand or so letters that will some day presumably enter the archives. Agacinski did not make herself available for interviews, but did confirm a timeline. Son Pierre regrets that his half brother, Daniel, did not attend their father's funeral, although he was not invited. Derrida was buried in a private secular ceremony in the Paris suburb of Ris-Orangis, site since 1968 of the family home. For his part, Daniel Agacinski, who never properly met his father, earned his agrégation in philosophy in 2007 at ENS. Marguerite Derrida, it turns out, counseled her husband to recognize this child officially, which he quietly did in 1986. During an interview, Pierre offered a frank assessment of his father: "There was in the temperament of my father, however open and audacious on the majority of things, some very archaic elements which we could not discuss" (580). Derrida evidently had other extramarital relationships hinted at but undocumented in the biography. We are left to speculate Derrida was perhaps a critic of monogamy. In the biographer's uncharacteristically bold words, Derrida "remained a grand seducer" and a person "capable of numerous fidelities" (516).

Of the 32 chapters composing the biography, one stands out dramatically from all the rest. Titled "Portrait of the Philosopher at 60," it suddenly stops following chronology and compiles a portrait of Derrida in the round. It takes 25 chapters and 500 pages to arrive at this summative account of distinctive features, eccentricities, and quirky personality traits done up very much in the style of popular biographies of great men. Derrida, for example, was a reckless car driver, unmindful of money, fond of ocean swimming, avidly watched television, was a doting parent and a jealous husband, had superstitions and phobias. He was extremely punctual and expected the same from others. Early in his career (but not before), he became something of a dandy in dress. One of his acquaintances depicts this trait as "radiant narcissism." About the time he got his first computer in 1986, a Mac which his children helped him master, Derrida's fame was such that his characteristic copious and attentive letter writing became nearly impossible; he relied more and more on the telephone. He no doubt found it increasingly difficult to keep up with requests for recommendations, project deadlines, complimentary works received, invitations, and so on. He had neither a regular secretary nor assistant. While he was an extremely fast keyboardist, Derrida tended to handwrite first drafts. His handwriting was almost indecipherable so much so that two of the 70 photos in the biography picture his scribbles, one early one late. From a private diary we learn Derrida fretted about his Algerian accent. Whatever else he might have been, Derrida was a mortal with flaws, quirks, and complexes including lousy handwriting and a regional twang.

Though buried, the central motif in this biography is *de trop*: Derrida as a person of too much, too many, outright excess. This trait pertains perhaps most notoriously to his scholarly articles, often extending to 100 printed pages, as well as his guest lectures lasting two or more uninterrupted hours of reading with rare eye contact. In short, there were too many books, articles three times normal length, marathon lectures, too much travel, innumerable contacts to maintain, endless situations requiring a response, and continuous overwork. The excess over the decades only increased. It's worth recalling that Derrida launched his career with three books in 1967, not the usual one or the unusual two: *La Voix et le phénomène*, *De la grammatologie*, and *L'Écriture et la différence*. He repeated the performance in 1972 with *La Dissémination, Marges—de la philosophie*, and *Positions*. In retrospect, such excess was the norm with Derrida. This remains an undeveloped yet amply illustrated major theme in his life and work that puts to rest the vestigial image of philosophy as a leisure activity.

The odd title of the first chapter is "Le Négus." It was a family term of affection given to Jackie in early childhood: his skin was then so dark, especially after sun exposure, almost like a Negro's skin. Right from the outset the author quietly and convincingly portrays Derrida as an outsider in this case like Ethiopian royalty (négus). But he offers no commentary on the African theme and too little on the outsider motif. He allows himself very few moments of broad speculation and judgment, adhering closely to a policy of just the facts based on very extensive interviews and archival research. The biographer rarely goes out on a limb and when he does so such moments are more like indulgences than slips. At the end of Part I, for instance, he ventures, "Beyond familial and personal wounds, the Algerian War constitutes also one of the sources of all his political thinking" (157). The problem here is not the conjecture, but the nearly complete absence of such suggestive observations and inferences. The ratio of detail to generalization is disproportionate in this enormous biography. It sometimes reads like a courtroom document surreptitiously fending off potential counterclaims from critics and enemies.

At a few turns, the author defends and at others he criticizes his subject, yet always rarely, quietly, and only in passing. They are peculiar instances. For example, to the mid-1980s growing complaints from French intellectuals about Derrida's increasing hermeticism and unreadability, he responds by citing an obscure reviewer in a small magazine, soon defunct, defending Derrida (Catherine David in *L'Autre Journal*, May 1986). While the biographer sympathizes with the reviewer's defense of Derrida's excessive close reading in our era of Attention Deficit Disorder and distracted reading, he does so only indirectly. An unprecedented event occurs when the author near the end of the final chapter proffers his personal opinion of a work by Derrida: "*Apprendre à vivre enfin* (2005) is a superb and limpid text, perhaps the best of introductions to his oeuvre" (655). This is a first, a firm personal judgment, plus an enthusiastic one at that, though of a minor work. At one point in a footnote, the author crosschecks and corrects a small error in Derrida's memory by citing a letter he had written twenty years earlier. Otherwise Derrida goes uncorrected in a book with over 1,300 footnotes. About Derrida's recognition and admission of de Man's anti-Semitism, expressed in the latter's most notorious wartime article, the biographer castigates very mildly "That does not prevent Derrida from undertaking 'close reading' of the article in question with somewhat excessive ingenuity and generosity" (484). "Somewhat." If you're looking for ideology or culture critique in this book, you've come to the wrong place.

Benoît Peeters's *Derrida* is a very broadly researched narrowly focused biography accessible to the educated non-specialist reader. It recounts the main and innumerable minor facts of Derrida's life without theatricalizing or idealizing or belittling. Derrida emerges as a singular human being rather than a representative man, or exemplary character, or genius-hero. The biographer appears a fair-minded outsider, who does not take sides, moralize, or blame. Readers should perhaps be grateful for this reserve. Nor does Peeters seek for an identity theme or the inner being or soul of Jacques Derrida. No, his two main interests reside in Derrida's long and rich professional life and in academic institutions and their folkways as experienced from Derrida's perspective. He shows very little interest in Derrida's philosophy or in its interpretation. Of course, many such inquiries already exist, more than enough doubtlessly in the biographer's view.

However, the biographer unfortunately does not delve into some of the expected spheres of life and academe. Although he does provide telling glimpses of Derrida's family life, he omits, for instance, family finances. Like Derrida himself, he does not talk about personal finances or money: this much of privacy remains. Did Derrida ever experience class-consciousness? I for one suppose so. What kind of sales did his works have? Apparently, not many books sold well except for the 100,000 threshold gradually exceeded by *De la grammatologie*. Nor is much offered about religion. From the 1970s onwards deconstruction was a transnational phenomenon, and Derrida was a global figure supported by inner and outer circles. Since Peeters writes unselfconsciously from a metropolitan Parisian perspective, he offers only the tiniest cameos in passing of Derrida's French and occasionally of his Anglophone coteries. Moreover, they are treated as influential individuals rather than academic networks.

John Updike once quipped that a biography is a "novel with index." Peeters's biography of Jacques Derrida is more like a sequence of numerous news stories minus a concept index. It holds back on empathy and vividness. This is odd coming from Peeters, a mid-career novelist, comic strip author, and cultural critic. There is no humor in the biography except once and inadvertently when wife Marguerite, in the course of an interview with the author, depicts husband Jacques's jealous temperament: "He wasn't happy when he failed to reach me right away. At every moment he wanted to know where I was, what I did and with whom. But if I had the misfortune of asking him a similar question, he replied: 'Ah, always this reciprocity'" (518).

It turns out Jacques Derrida was a hoarder, excessively so, saving every scrap of paper over the course of his life, starting in adolescence. This material includes innumerable letters, graded school papers, personal notebooks, drafts of work, seminar lectures, plus documents about him like reviews, newspaper items, and scholarly texts. The biographer consulted this material, interviewed 100 or so people, and examined audio and videotapes. He explains the process of immersion in a fast-paced side project, *Trois ans avec Derrida: Les Carnets d'un biographe*, published simultaneously with the biography by Flammarion. Not at all incidentally, Derrida's main publisher, Galilée, announced plans in 2008 to publish the 40 plus volumes of his yearly seminars covering the period from 1960 to 2003. A distinctive feature of the theory renaissance is this archival turn. Another symptomatic element is the many celebrity-style biographies, autobiographies, and memoirs of recent decades. Given the revelations in the Derrida biography, there will be a massive future flood of his publications beyond the seminars. In this wave it will be letters, notebooks, and tapes. Other leading French theorists will almost certainly be subjects of similar treatment.

8

Postmodernism revisited

I've been surprised to see a spate of books and articles on postmodernism published in the second decade of the twenty-first century. Following its highpoint in the 1990s, marked by the publication of Fredric Jameson's landmark book, *Postmodernism, or the Cultural Logic of Late Capitalism* (1991), interest in this topic has gradually waned only to come back now. It's a question of survivance. This return has me wondering what is living and what is dead in theories of postmodernism?

Earlier segmentations into "early" and "late" postmodernism feel very dated and crude now. Oddly, much recent work on postmodernism finely segments the era but without saying so. My argument in this chapter is not only that we still reside in the postmodern era with no end in sight, but also that we need to sharply segment the period for it to be more explanatory, relevant, and useful.

The term "postmodern" has long been employed in three different yet overlapping ways—as a style, a philosophy or movement, and a period. It's not unusual to encounter talk of postmodern architecture, painting, or cuisine backed up with a list of distinctive stylistic features. The canonical trait of postmodern architecture is pastiche, of postmodern painting appropriation, of postmodern cuisine fusion. Historical recycling and remixing are the primary cultural modes. For philosophers, however, postmodernism signifies French poststructuralism, mainly works by Jean Baudrillard, Gilles Deleuze, Jacques Derrida, Michel Foucault, Julia Kristeva, and Jean-François Lyotard, with special emphasis on the transformation of reality into images, floating signifiers, and simulations disseminated by ever more ubiquitous media screens and spectacles. For their part, cultural critics construe postmodernism as a period spanning from the 1960s, 1970s, or 1980s up to the present (or alternatively ending in the 1990s) distinguished by, for example, the dramatic erosion of the traditional high/low cultural distinction, the implosion of disciplinary autonomies, the rise of numerous innovative new social movements, and the global spread of extreme laissez-faire economics. In the latter scenario, postmodern times describe an eclectic postindustrial era of pluralism and disaggregation, of hybrids and fusions, accompanied unsurprisingly by nostalgia, retro currents, and backlashes. The period concept has long encompassed postmodern style and postmodern philosophy following Jameson's widely accepted broad usage. Very often the term "postmodernity" serves as a synonym for "postmodernism."

What is missing now is a sense of the distinct phases of the postmodern period. In retrospect, the years 1973, 1989, 2001, and 2011 stand out as important turning points. The first, 1973, designates the establishment of a new global monetary regime of floating currencies marking a shift away from Keynesian Welfare State economics. From this moment on, postmodern financialization characteristic of late capitalism takes off. The second, 1989, involves the dissolution of the USSR and the advent of the New World Order with the attendant redrawing of maps and alliances. It's a moment of triumphant globalized consumer capitalism and Empire. The third, 2001, signals the onset of Empire's endless global war on terror accompanied by ubiquitous surveillance as well as the spread of anti-globalization movements, progressive and regressive. With its many Occupy movements and its many worldwide national street-incited revolutions, 2011 inaugurates a fourth phase of the postmodern era characterized by growing demands for political freedom, social justice, and economic fairness. Modernity spanned 200 years so why shouldn't postmodernity exceed the few decades often hastily allotted to it?

As a period concept, postmodernism continues to do useful work today. In its absence contemporary history appears haphazard, chaotic, and atomized. This period framing foregrounds significant patterns and themes, both positive and negative. In the event, it most famously highlights, for example, the promotion of difference over sameness as in ongoing multicultural and diversity projects; the decentering of identity into multiple subject positions and the increasing volatilization and plasticity of the body; plus the interactions and tensions between micro and macro narratives and phenomena such as electrified national fences against immigrants versus borderless global flows of money, information, and goods. Well-known and still pertinent keywords depicting the postmodern era over the decades include "heterogeneity," "uneven development," "dissensus," "incommensurability," "hybridity," and "deregulation." By common agreement, the dominant aesthetic form of the period remains assemblage. Social constructionism is the dominant epistemology. On one hand, the postmodern age is a time of widespread dehierarchizations and disaggregations; on the other, it displays unifying patterns and themes captured in the paradoxical master term "heterogeneity." The periodizing concept continues to facilitate cognitive mapping and cultural generalizations particularly in this case of postmodernism where disorganization is the main mode of its cultural logic.

I am aware that some critics in certain fields, such as architecture and fiction, believe postmodernism came to an end during the 1980s and 1990s. They have sought to name what comes after— for example, altermodernism, cosmodernism, digimodernism, metamodernism, transmodernism—with little success and less agreement. To them, I would say try treating postmodernism not as an ephemeral vanguard style but an ongoing historical period characterized precisely by a panoply of styles, old, new, and mixed.

When we turn to recent works on the postmodern era, what do we find? To begin with, it's a moment of consolidation and taking stock rooted in a strong sense of postmodernism's continuing relevance as a discrete historical period. This buttressing, however, very much divides the history of postmodernization by area and field. Not surprisingly, it's a matter of assembled and aggregated micro histories such as one finds in *The Routledge Companion to Postmodernism*, Third Edition (2011), edited by Stuart Sim. This casebook is a representative conspectus by many hands covering in a dozen and a half chapters separate domains that range from postmodern politics, religion, and postcolonial studies to art, architecture, and cinema to fiction, theory, and popular culture to technoscience, organizational theory, and international relations to feminism, sexuality studies, and lifestyles to music, television, and performance studies, with philosophy receiving pride of place yet equal time. This historical account, I note in passing, omits postmodern poetry, cuisine, and globalization studies, not to mention many other areas of culture and society. But the proliferation of micro narratives and petits récits illustrates both the continuing pertinence of the postmodern concept and its characteristic disorganized form. It also suggests the enduring heuristic power of the concept. Nowadays the argument that postmodernism is over strikes me as an unconvincing countercurrent troubled by the absence of anything to take its place, even though I realize many critics are bored with the concept and wish for something new.

When confronting the question about how things stand now with postmodernism, literary and cultural critic Ihab Hassan, a pioneer on postmodernism, offers the following reply in his essay "Beyond Postmodernism" published in 2010: "What lies beyond postmodernism? In the larger scheme, postmodernity looms, looms with its multiple crises of identity, with its diasporas and genocides, with its desperate negotiations between local practices and global procedures" (138). According to Hassan, there is no end to postmodernism. However, in recent years it has undergone dire globalization and a name change to postmodernity. For him, globalization represents a key, yet undated turning point linked clearly to the new century's global wars of terror. Late in his career, Hassan turns to ethics and to spirituality in response to what he continues to identify as postmodern culture, a surprisingly indispensable historical frame, he admits.

Another pioneering scholar of postmodernism, Charles Jencks, observes in the first sentence of his *Story of Post-Modernism* (2011): "Since the Millennium Post-Modernism, in all but name, has returned as a major movement in the arts" (9). On his opening page he discusses "re-emergent themes" that have evolved over 50 years of this "resurgent tradition." In addition, to map the history and phases of postmodern architecture, he offers a detailed evolutionary chart that identifies on a timeline from 1960 to 2010 dozens of trends, major works, leading figures, plus key locations (48–49). In his setup to the map, Jencks notes that postmodernism "has enjoyed a most surprising burst of strength since the year 2000" (47). The problem with Jencks is that he limits postmodernism to the arts.

Realizing that he can neither scrap the postmodern concept nor name a new period, Jeffery Nealon symptomatically portrays recent times in the wake of some other critics as a "post-postmodern" era. How is it described and how do things stand here with postmodernism? According to Nealon's *Post-Postmodernism or, the Cultural Logic of Just-in-Time Capitalism* (2012), "Postmodernism is not a thing of the past, any more than the 1980s are, precisely because it's hard to understand today as anything other than an intensified version of yesterday" (8). Indeed. As Nealon notes, today we have more capitalist commodification, more multinational corporatizations, and more speculative financial instruments like derivatives (swaps, options, futures). If this intensification surprises and upsets you, argues Nealon, you're postmodern, but if you're clued into this hyperreality you're post-postmodern. In any event, Nealon does not dump the postmodern concept, quite the opposite.

What characterizes post-postmodernism for Jeffrey Nealon are not only intensification of postmodernism, but also attitude adjustment from shock to cool, yet still critical, pragmatic acknowledgment. Nealon's perception of post-postmodernism as really hyperpostmodernism, to give it a more accurate name, reflects a preference for change within rather than outside or against the system. In elaborating his argument, he memorably depicts the post-postmodern corporate university and the role of theory in unexpectedly positive ways. Why? There's no sense being upset or cynical at this late point; it's better to work for change within the terms of the system. What distinguishes Nealon's post-postmodernism is pragmatism more equable than the 1980s engagé neopragmatism of Richard Rorty or the cynical version of Stanley Fish. Here's a telling example. The post-postmodern English Department should reimagine and market itself as what it has already become, argues Nealon in a self-consciously practical way, a diversified corporation with multiple investments beyond its core businesses and with an innovative R&D wing (theory). The department is very much in sync with the times unlike the broader corporate university, which is anachronistically overstuffed with managers and needs downsizing in those ranks.

Where does theory stand? For Nealon its fostering of critical thinking, problem solving, and innovation will insure a thriving future. The postmodern corporate university, after all, "has been very, very good to theory, feminism, gender studies, cultural studies, poststructuralism, postcolonialism, African American studies, visual culture, and the like ... " (81–82). Furthermore, the post-postmodern corporate university promises a better future for theory and English studies given that innovation is its prime directive. However, argues Nealon, theory and the English Department need to jettison some particular baggage from the past.

As long as anyone can remember, theory in English Departments has focused on and justified its existence by interpreting cultural artifacts, uncovering textual meanings, and sharpening hermeneutic approaches, that is, close reading. Certainly that was the case at the outset of the postmodern period, but the tide started going out on this narrow mission in the fin de siècle marked especially by the spread of cultural studies. Nowadays the focus on interpretation, warns Nealon, is "the road to nowhere" (124). Admonitions follow. Beware theorists. Give up looking for the next big approach or method linked to interpretation. Get over your funk and posttheory malaise. "And if there's no 'next big thing' coming down the theory pike, it's precisely because such a notion of the 'next big thing' (like feminism, deconstruction, or new historicism in their day) has tended to mean the arrival of a new interpretive paradigm. The primary reason there's no dominant post-postmodern interpretive paradigm on the horizon is not so much because of the exhaustion of theory itself (I can immediately think of a dozen underexplored interpretive models or theorists), but because the work of interpretation is no longer the primary research work of literature departments" (133). The way Nealon convincingly construes matters all talk of "posttheory," "after theory," and "theory exhaustion" marks not the end of postmodernism or of theory but the dramatic swerve away from texts to their contexts. Although misunderstood, this turn is a good change, insuring a future for theory and for English departments provided there's no backsliding to the paradigm of textual interpretation and the consequent reduction of theory to interpretive approaches. The project to resuscitate exclusive close reading is a wrong turn.

Oddly, Jeffrey Nealon makes no mention of the many recent calls to return to close reading. He does parenthetically highlight the theory renaissance underway. But where Nealon himself goes wrong with his admonitions is in advocating a stark modernist either/or instead of a postmodernist both/and choice when it comes to interpretation versus contextualization (see Hutcheon 2007 on both/and as paradigmatically postmodern). It would be a mistake to rule out the projects of interpretation, of contextualization, or of theoretical speculation. Multitasking and heterogeneity distinguish contemporary conditions in English departments.

I have another criticism of Nealon. While I concur that the university has accepted theory and its many wings from feminism and ethnic studies to postcolonial theory and cultural studies, I need to register a serious reservation. Most universities to this day underfund gender and ethnic studies, relying on part-time staff, donated labor, and inadequate facilities for interdisciplinary studies. The typical organizational form is the program not the department. Programs lack full-time faculty, ample office space, and substantial budgets. Despite such programs' successes with students and faculty, there are very few departments as opposed to many programs of, for instance, women's studies or cultural studies. The program form offers not only flimsy infrastructure, but also dirt-cheap recognition from the twenty-first-century corporate university.

Without saying so, Nealon's work underscores two key phases of postmodernism that impact theory: the 1990s turn away from textual interpretation to cultural studies and the early twenty-first-century intensification of the corporate university. Both of these phenomena involve the repurposing of theory. It's good news for theorists purportedly. However, Nealon plays down while admitting crucial facts on the ground, specifically faculty downsizing, student indenture, and the rise of critical university studies (a new energetic branch of institutional critique). And again, he ignores the many disparate calls to return to close reading, seemingly a new phase of long-standing antitheory countercurrents.

To sum up, Jeffrey Nealon twists himself into productive knots in trying to answer the question what comes after postmodernism. To his considerable credit, he doesn't stop at the usual dismissive "postmodernism is over." It has morphed into post-postmodernism, which is hyperpostmodernism. There is no after postmodernism.

In a similar case, Christian Moraru in his *Cosmodernism: American Narrative, Late Globalization, and the New Cultural Imaginary* (2011) argues at length for labeling the period from 1989 to the present cosmodernism, but symptomatically he has trouble jettisoning postmodernism. On his final page he observes astutely: "Nor is postmodernism 'over'" (316).

A parallel line of argumentation is very plainly stated by Hutcheon and her coauthors in the opening sentence of the updated entry on postmodernism in *The Princeton Encyclopedia of Poetry and Poetics*, Fourth Edition (2012): "The definition and history of postmodernism have both been highly contested; postmodernism was declared dead shortly after it came into being, yet it appears to be still with us" (1095). The entry enumerates and discusses without hesitations salient features of postmodern poetry. At the outset it carefully notes the existence of different as well as uneven developments across the arts and sciences and within each area. The upshot is that plural poetries constitute postmodern poetry. In my terms, the postmodern disaggregation of the poetry field persists well into the twenty-first century. This claim is especially borne out across the thousand pages of *Postmodern American Poetry: A Norton Anthology*, 2nd edition (2013), edited by Paul Hoover, who concludes his introduction: "We should not imagine that a single style rules the period, such as language poetry, conceptual poetry, or the postlanguage lyric. It is all of the above" (lvi). Where the encyclopedia's account comes up short is in not explicitly considering phases or key turning points in the fifty-year history of postmodern poetry. For example, it skirts the 1970s emergence of LANGUAGE poetry in the wake of confessional poetry's dire expressivism. Nor does it mention the 1980s and 1990s rise of popular poetries such as slam and rap pitched against the background of the academic Creative Writing establishment and its official verse culture. Nothing is said about the maturation of born-digital electronic poetry in the twenty-first century nor its archives online with the Electronic Literature Organization.

Here is an additional parallel case study but from another field, art history. When he comes in 2011 to characterize the sphere of contemporary painting and particularly twenty-first-century work, leading art critic Barry Schwabsky labels it very persuasively a "pluralist era" (11). Not surprisingly, he initially sets the contemporary period against the earlier high modernist programs of aesthetic purification propounded by dogmatic postwar advocates of abstract art so famously contested by 1960s pop artists and fellow travelers. Thus Claes Oldenburg over against Ad Reinhardt marks for Schwabsky the onset of postmodern painting. Helpfully, he depicts three turning points in postmodern history, yet without naming them as such. One is the 1960s and 1970s shift away from art for art's sake to everyday life in its political, erotic, and mystical configurations, a transformation that persists today. The second is the continuous yet intensifying impact on figurative painting of our changing visual culture most notably film, television, video, photography (analogue and digital), and the Internet. Here representation and simulation become increasingly entangled, when not indistinguishable. The third is the recent crowd sourcing involved in Phaidon's publication of the landmark Vitamin Series, particularly *Vitamin P* (2002) and *Vitamin P2* (2011), both of which tomes Schwabsky had a hand in. With an introduction by Schwabsky, *Vitamin P2* contains from three to five color plates by 115 newly prominent international painters nominated by 77 art critics and historians. It displays a staggering array of styles from abstract to figurative to conceptual to multimodal painting. This is postmodern pluralism writ large. It answers definitively the recurring contemporary question "Is painting a dying art?" Not incidentally, the twenty-first-century Vitamin Series consists of four additional parallel tomes on today's drawing, photography, sculpture and installation, plus design and architecture, all similarly focused on contemporary work and all crowd sourced. It's a postmodern project par excellence without the label. It encompasses many incompatible styles within separate areas of the arts, testifying to twenty-first-century proliferation as well as disaggregation in the arts.

What characterizes postmodernism yesterday and today is a persistent disorganization of culture into separate spheres and the ubiquitous interaction, sometimes convergence, of the fields. It has been going on long enough that we can and should distinguish phases of development in each domain. At the same time there are culture-wide phenomena affecting the separate spheres in particular ways. I have in mind the well-attested worldwide intensification, transformation, and spread of media, popular culture, democracy movements, religious awakenings, and wars as well as free-market fundamentalism. It's a matter of scale, that is, of globally interacting micro and macro narratives, plus uneven developments and convergences, operating often simultaneously. On one hand, we experience the mishmash of world music and cuisines and, on the other, uniformities of globalization and Empire popping up everywhere like Coca-Cola and reality TV subgenres. The postmodern concept captures these cultural motions and scales effectively in a way that no contending notion does. Still, I believe we need more systematic and explicit analyses of phases given the unanticipated longevity of the period.

Part of rehistoricizing postmodernism involves critiques of postmodernity as well as modernity. Critical histories, early and numerous, have come from every conceivable spot on the spectrum of cultural politics with more doubtlessly to come. Key instances and insightful criticisms against postmodern society and culture include nonstop critiques of the shortcomings and depredations of late capitalism; the cannibalizations and ironic mashups of cultural histories (treated as supermarkets); the posthumanist divisiveness stemming from identity politics and multiculturalism; the fragmentations of contemporary antinomian micropolitics and new social movements; the degeneration of standards in the celebration of popular culture and assemblage aesthetics; the ecological damages due to unregulated technosciences; plus the dominant intellectual combination of cultural relativism—social constructionism—standpoint epistemology that undermines truth. This list could be lengthened, to be sure. As a historical concept, postmodernism includes critiques not just celebrations and impartial descriptions of it. One last point against recurring homogenization—the onset, configuration, and critical reception of the postmodern era differ from one nation to another, as published studies of postmodern China, Japan, Russia, and the United States make clear.

During the contemporary period, theory came into its own as a distinct academic postmodern field. In my view, it has gone through five phases. First, theory was initially institutionalized beginning in the late 1960s and into the 1970s through a remarkable proliferation of theory-designated journals and the establishment of the School of Criticism and Theory. Second, many academic theory programs and curricular tracks emerged during the 1980s while university and commercial presses started churning out numerous theory books. This decade also witnessed a boom in the academic theory job market and an upsurge of antitheory sentiments. From then on academics in the humanities and social sciences felt it necessary to add to their professional profiles an explicit theory component. Third, beginning in the 1990s, theory innovations had less to do with major schools and movements—as they did throughout the twentieth century—and more to do with the creation of dozens of semiautonomous subfields such as trauma studies, body studies, and whiteness studies. This is the moment some critics labeled "posttheory" to separate it from the previous decade of "grand theory." As my map of the Twenty-First-Century Literary and Cultural Theory Renaissance illustrates, theory in the new century is a disaggregated field loosely organized around key topics, some perennial, some contemporary. In this sense, it has a distinctively postmodern form, as I have argued throughout this book. Fourth, the continuing spread in the new century of the corporate university, home to theory, has generated symptomatic responses, positive and negative, ranging from the formation of critical university studies to retrenchment to close reading to the defensive consolidation of the field via monumentalizing textbooks like the *Norton Anthology of Theory and Criticism* and others. Fifth, the major accomplishments of earlier phases of development continued into the second decade of the new century. More or less thriving, for example, are theory journals and book publications, the School of Criticism and Theory, academic theory courses and programs, and the requirement of adding a theory designation to one's professional identity. And the proliferation of new subfields gives no signs of petering out.

The postmodern upsurge of theory continues. The calls for close reading and textual interpretation coming recently from prominent theorists appear less as hostile antitheory groundswells and more as defensive returns to critical approaches and methods long steeped in the history of Western criticism and theory from the ancient Greeks to the present. A sixth phase of postmodern theory is emerging. Textbooks, teaching, and publications have very recently started to reach beyond European traditions to African, Arabic, Chinese, Persian, South Asian, and other traditions of theory. Postmodernism lives on and continues to evolve. Sure to come, its end is not yet in sight.

9

Twenty-first-century theory favorites

There are a number of groundbreaking books, favorites of mine, which, taken together, provide a suggestive panorama of the twenty-first-century theory renaissance, particularly in its symptomatic preoccupations with globalizing neoliberal economics, identity politics, and the corporate university. Most of these books are best sellers pitched at general audiences with theorists in the role of public intellectuals.

First on all lists is doubtlessly Michael Hardt and Antonio Negri's bestselling *Empire* (2000). Its main contributions come with its influential conception of the multitude, its account of immaterial labor, and its portrait of Empire as the latest form of global hegemony. In place of the masses, the crowd, the people, or the working class, Hardt and Negri put the multitude. Like the later 99% versus the 1% of the 2011 Occupy movements, the multitude names the worldwide multipolar collective, real and potential, solidified yet scattered in resistance to the intensifying global capitalist order. Here resistance takes the form of both antagonism and autonomy. Immaterial labor, following upon industrial manual labor, designates the combined intellectual-affective work increasingly characteristic of the service economy. As the leading edge, it models the coming future of work and challenges contending residual modes. Characteristic and recognizable negative features of the new labor practices include (1) eroding the 8 hour workday (being on call 24/7), (2) valuing mobility and flexibility particularly through temporary contracts, and (3) rendering work precarious, for example, through deunionization and shedding benefits. "Empire" is the term Hardt and Negri famously use to depict postcolonial and post-Cold War globalization that promotes not only the rapid movement across borders of money, information, technology, products, and people, but also the ceding of considerable national sovereignty to supranational non-democratic institutions that increasingly regulate life. Well-known instances include the International Monetary Fund (IMF), World Bank (WB), World Trade Organization (WTO), United Nations, and the Groups of 8 and 20 as well as transnational corporations and nongovernmental organizations. Many cooperative nation-states belong here, as do central banks.

Narrowly construed, *Empire* carries out a retrofitting of Marxist criticism and theory for the new century. More broadly, it develops strong arguments about globalization for cultural theory, which the immediate and voluminous outpouring of responses to it signal. Among the earliest book-length collective responses are *Debating Empire* (2003), edited by Gopal Balakrishnan; *Empire's New Clothes* (2004), compiled by Paul Passavant and Jodi Dean; Negri plus Hardt's own second-round *Reflections on Empire* (2003; trans. 2008); and the extended critique of Atilio Bóron, *Empire and Imperialism* (2005). Much more reaction has followed these immediate substantial responses. *Empire* remains a major work of the new century.

Of the twenty sections of *Empire*, none is more obviously pertinent to the concerns of cultural theory than "Symptoms of Passage." Hardt and Negri here attack reigning accounts of postmodernism, postcolonial theory, and religious fundamentalisms. As is well known, both postcolonialism and postmodern philosophy criticize the errors of the past, specifically modern colonialism and Enlightenment modernity, while promoting contemporary hybridity, difference, and flexibility. But, note Hardt and Negri, the latter are the very values of today's corporate capitalism and the world market. So the theorists of the "post," cosmopolitan elites have been outflanked, misrecognizing the new forms of power, being too focused on the past rather than on the present and future. Similarly, Hardt and Negri construe fundamentalisms not as revivals of the premodern past but as refusals of the globalizing present. The ancient traditions championed by them are really inventions of the present. In their animus against modernity, fundamentalisms, both Christian and Muslim, share a certain postmodern frame of mind. But in Hardt and Negri's broad view, the usual "postmodernist discourses appeal primarily to the winners in the process of globalization and fundamentalist discourse to the losers" (150). From the perspective of cultural theory, they argue, postmodernism, postcolonialism, and present-day fundamentalisms all constitute significant sentinels, symptoms, of the passage on the way to globalization in the age of Empire.[1]

Like other admiring readers of *Empire*, I have some reservations. As a critic, I am obliged to weigh the strengths and the weaknesses of the work. Hardt and Negri too readily dismiss national sovereignty in their depiction of the transnational supersovereignty of global institutions such as the IMF and WB. Also, they reduce both postmodern and postcolonial theories to the critique of traditional binary concepts underlying the Enlightenment and to the advocacy of abstract differences. Nevertheless, they note that we are living in a historical period persuasively and repeatedly named by them "postmodernity." As I see it, they dispatch the archaisms of fundamentalisms too easily. And for me their tone is off: while the flipside of the developing global world market is the forming multitude (a communism to come), their hope for this countervailing utopian force feels overly optimistic. All that said, *Empire* has effectively reenergized leftist cultural theory, challenged postcolonial and postmodern philosophical theory, and sharpened plus broadened critique of the juridico-political institutions and practices of globalization.

Perhaps the most striking academic book in the area of recent contemporary minority identity studies is Craig Womack's little-noticed *Red on Red: Native American Literary Separatism* (1999). As a Muskogee Creek and Cherokee Indian, Womack advocates national tribal sovereignty against both synthetic pan-tribalism and globalization theory. There are more than 500 federally recognized tribes in the US, spanning many different geographies, cultures, and languages. Womack's opening chapter provides an account of the history, government, and religion of the Creek nation. It has a population of 40,000 today. This is followed by a chapter not

---

[1] "The coming Empire is not American and the United States is not its center.... The United States certainly occupies a privileged position in the global segmentations and hierarchies of Empire" (Hardt and Negri, 384). This controversial assessment is intensely contested. See, for example, Bóron.

only criticizing the pan-tribalism of mainstream social sciences and humanities, but simultaneously reclaiming the distinctive traditions and motifs of the Creek nation. Next comes an illustrative chapter analyzing the Creek oral story of Turtle, which is transcribed into the native language and accompanied for contrast by several English translations. Womack then mounts an unsparing critique of Creek author Alice Callahan's 1890s novel *Wynema* as an assimilationist and Christian supremacist tract written for a white audience. He turns thereafter to separate chapters of appreciative analysis of Creek authors Alexander Posey, Louis Oliver, and Joy Harjo, plus to conclude gay Cherokee writer Lynn Riggs.

Given his primary Native American audience, Womack registers but doesn't rehearse in detail the traumatic history of European invasion, genocide, colonization, removal (diaspora), racism, language eradication, and land theft. Along the way he debunks the popular cultural stereotypes of the Indian as noble savage, stoic warrior, nature-loving mystic, lazy full blood, tragic figure, and vanishing American. As a self-identified queer Creek Cherokee Indian, Womack holds firmly to an essentialist view of identity grounded in life-sustaining difference. "Behind the liberal 'why can't we all just get along?' line of reasoning, often applied to race as well, is an underlying supremacism, a demand that everybody be white and heterosexual, that cultural identities be sacrificed so that dominant culture can rest safely" (300–301). Womack's separatism, hostile to ideas of assimilation, is wary of Europeanized postcolonial theory. He regards American tribes as living today under decidedly colonial not postcolonial conditions.

Red on Red adds a new dimension to subaltern race and ethnicity studies by casting the Native American aesthetic as a factitious white liberal construct. The book is critical of broad general categories— disembodied syntheses—characteristic of globalized theory such as academic indigenous studies, Anglophone literature, postcolonial theory, and Native American culture. It is, moreover, an instance of the twenty-first-century rebirth of US literature as multilingual memorably advanced in the *Multilingual Anthology of American Literature: A Reader of Original Texts with English Translations* (2000), edited by Harvard Professors Marc Shell and Werner Sollors. In addition, *Red on Red* is a distinctive blend of scholarship and intimate critique written resolutely from a first-person point of view, a mode pioneered by other minority scholars in the 1980s and thereafter.

Another distinctive feature that sets *Red on Red* apart, and that represents one path of theory, is that it is a kind of creative criticism from novelist Womack. The book contains eight fictional letters scattered across the work as interchapters written often in dialect by Creek Jim Chibbo to Hotgun (a Creek full-blood traditionalist), both fictional characters. The letters cover a wide range of topics, tones, and genres, mashing up Creek history, literary criticism, and popular culture.

Last but not least, *Red on Red* repeatedly returns to the land, specifically the details of Muskogee Creek land. It's less an ecocritical concern with the environment than a tribal commitment to land-based collective identity, sovereignty, and survival. "The importance to this kind of place-specific writing, I believe, is, in fact, increasing over time…because the land provides a constant against cultural deterioration. No matter what happens with language and culture, the land remains if jurisdiction over it is protected, which means that tribes always…continue if a relationship to the land is still possible" (171). Not surprisingly, *Red on Red* is preoccupied with homecoming and retribalization more than migration, diaspora, or mobility so fundamental to globalization theory.

Within Native American specialist circles, *Red on Red* elicited immediate spirited criticisms to its tribalcentrism and initiated a major controversy. It started with Elvira Pulitano's *Toward a Native American Critical Theory* (2003), followed by the collective responses gathered both in *American Indian Literary Nationalism* (2006) by Jace Weaver (Cherokee), Craig Womack, and Robert Warrior (Osage) and then in *Reasoning Together* (2008) by the Native Critics Collective (a group of twelve authors). My own criticism of the book concerns its understandable yet dispiriting avoidance of relevant contemporary theory movements, for example, indigenous studies, cultural studies, postcolonial theory, and queer theory. This avoidance is less an example of antitheory than a determined reliance on tribal resources. Also Womack's book adheres to an inside/outside binary that leaves scant room for mixed bloods not to mention fellow travelers like myself. It has nothing to say about social class. Whether this omission is simply an oversight or a tactic, it misses a key topic of concern in the new post-1988 era of proliferating American Indian gambling casinos and the resulting exorbitant amassing of wealth by a few select tribes.

The most pointed and passionate twenty-first-century critique of identity theory from an academic literary critic appears in Walter Benn Michaels's *The Trouble with Diversity: How We Learned to Love Identity and Ignore Inequality* (2006). About nationalistic tribalism like Womack's, Michaels complains angrily: "New forms of 'ancient' identities are being invented every day. And the function of all of them is to provide people with ways of thinking about themselves that have as little as possible to do with either their material circumstances or their political ideals" (160). In the name of economic fairness and justice, Michaels criticizes as distraction all talk of difference, multiculturalism, affirmative action, and cultural resistance. What matters in present circumstances is class not culture.

Unlike his earlier works of literary criticism published by university presses, Michaels's jeremiad is a fast-paced trade book aimed at the American public. It is an iconoclastic effort to revive US left populism from a non-Marxist pragmatic position. *The Trouble with Diversity* is arguably the best example early in the new century of a book by a distinguished liberal literature professor metamorphosed self-consciously into a public intellectual. It is reminiscent of mid-twentieth-century non-academic discourse from the New York intellectuals not the New Historicism with which Michaels is firmly associated. Tellingly, it does not concern itself with globalization but with national political economic conditions and the American university.

The main target of Michaels's book is post-Cold War capitalism in the US, specifically growing inequality and its role in national education, health care, law, politics, and culture. Disappointingly, he does not suggest any political programs, or question national sovereignty or, worse yet, figure in the forces of globalization. Also he presents a too stark either/or for theory and criticism—*either* focus on class *or* on race, gender, and sexuality (identity). A choice of both/and would work much better than this shortsighted either/ or tactic of smart polemic. As leading American philosopher Nancy Fraser has long eloquently argued, recognition and redistribution are both essential democratic social and political ideals. What Michaels does passionately is to excoriate the US academic left and right, the culture wars, and higher education's preoccupation with diversity. "American universities are propaganda machines that might as well have been designed to ensure that the class structure of American society remains unchallenged" (17).

While there are many critics of identity theory, none remains more antithetical than Giogio Agamben, especially in his famous book *Homo Sacer: Sovereign Power and Bare Life* (1995; trans. 1998). Agamben's conceptualization of "bare life" derives from ancient philosophy in Greece and Rome but updated to account for contemporary situations such as Nazi concentration camps, genocide in Rwanda, and rape compounds in former Yugoslavia. The foundation of the political, argues Agamben, is not the social contract, or the friend/enemy distinction, but the sovereign's declaration of a state of exception (which produces bare life). Bare life, this "originary political element" (90)—for example, the *homo sacer* in Rome, or the *sans papiers* in Europe, or the illegal combatants in Guantánamo Bay—is the real matrix of political theory and practice. Ever more obviously, as one critic observes, it's "the default status of any person whatsoever" (Shütz 96). The camp form is the key locus of bare life. Agamben's prophetic book precedes the US war on terror by six years. But it is this war that gives the book a second life at the dawn of the new century. The work foresees the spread of black sites of terror, maximum security prisons, and Abu Ghraib-style human rights violations. Stripped of law by a juridico-ethical ban (abandonment), a regular founding function of politics, bare life, an inclusive exclusion, precedes all features of identity. Here Agamben self-consciously and memorably politicizes Heidegger's phenomenological ontology of Dasein and recasts Foucault's biopolitics of carceral society no longer limited to modernity. Myself and other critics, however, are quick to point out Agamben's memorable account of bare life ignores contemporary inequalities, for example of race, gender, and sexuality, which constitute empowering bases for resistance undertaken by many powerful social movements. Moreover, its implicit desubjectivization of life, an unstated anarchist motif, sets aside all consideration of political economy.

Vociferous complaints from the 1970s onward about the rise of raw unregulated free-market capitalism, associated with the Reagan and Thatcher eras, spread in the fin de siècle and very broadly in the new century. While such complaints are clear in the work of Hardt and Negri and Michaels, though not with Womack or with

Agamben, it culminates in David Harvey's often and justly cited *A Brief History of Neoliberalism* (2005). Harvey's critical history of this fundamentalist strain of political economy famously first attracted notice in his landmark *The Condition of Postmodernity* (1989). But it is the later much less ponderous more pointed book addressed to a general audience that helped solidify, condense, and widely disseminate the critique of worldwide national neoliberalisms. From the present vantage point in the second decade of the new century, *Brief History* foresees the likely coming of the financial crash of September 2008. For North American and British literary and cultural critics, it is the most cited book on political economy in an era of innumerable such works. The whole area has and is undergoing a revival not seen since the 1930s. Among Harvey's most significant contributions are a comprehensive and convincing account of neoliberal theory and practice; an unabashed critique of the consequences and contradictions of neoliberalism; and a scrupulous attention to national differences in his cameo case studies of Mexico, Argentina, South Korea, Sweden, China, the UK, and the US.

David Harvey treats neoliberalism very convincingly as a global phenomenon with distinctive national features and histories. Here is how he defines it at the outset:

> Neoliberalism is in the first instance a theory of political economic practices that proposes that human well-being can best be advanced by liberating individual entrepreneurial freedoms and skills within an institutional framework characterized by strong private property rights, free markets, and free trade.... The state has to guarantee, for example, the quality and integrity of money. It must also set up those military, defence, police, and legal structures and functions required to secure private property rights.... Furthermore, if markets do not exist (in areas such as land, water, education, health care, social security, or environmental pollution) then they must be created, by state action if necessary. But beyond these tasks the state should not venture. (2)

Today there is little surprise in such neoliberal theory and practice. And that is a key point. Neoliberal doctrine has become hegemonic in nation after nation. It seems common sense that we encounter all the time. Historically speaking, it replaced the idea of the Welfare State that reigned from the 1930s to the 1960s. The Welfare State nowadays holds the status of a dying vestigial form. Across the globe, neoliberal governments withdraw from or reduce funding for social provisions such as higher education, health care, and pollution prevention. Instead they privatize medical care, tertiary education, and environmental safety. Typically, they auction to businesses that seek profits through commodification such goods and services as water, pollution rights, and hospital care. Costs get shifted onto individuals for higher education expenses, health insurance, and retirement funding. Other well-known policies of neoliberalism that Harvey highlights include low wages, low tax rates, and deregulation of industries, for example, banking, airlines, and telecommunications.

What's wrong with neoliberalism in Harvey's view? It creates a dog-eat-dog world of disposable workers, a small class of super wealthy elites, widespread social insecurity, rampant debt and bankruptcy, race-to-the-bottom outsourcing, shrinking middle classes, plutocracy, corporate welfare (for instance, bank bailouts), and explosive growth in rates of the working poor. He is particularly critical, memorably so, of financialization, which has displaced industrial production as a leading sector of economic growth. During the neoliberal era, the financial system has dramatically expanded its share of national economies and redistributed wealth upwards from public to private realms, which is especially clear in the US and UK:

> Deregulation allowed the financial system to become one of the main centers of redistributive activity through speculation, predation, fraud, and thievery. Stock promotions, ponzi schemes, structured asset destruction through inflation, asset-stripping through mergers and acquisitions, the promotion of levels of debt incumbency that reduced whole populations, even in the advanced capitalist countries, to debt peonage, to say nothing of corporate fraud, dispossession of assets (the raiding of pension funds and their decimation by stock and corporate collapses) by credit and stock manipulations—all of these became central features of the capitalist financial system. (161)

Harvey is especially critical of the practice of stock options replacing salary for top managers and CEOs. Why? They lead to preoccupation not with manufacturing and productivity but with short-term profitable stock bubbles. Outrageously high CEO pay comes to symbolize the financial dynamics of neoliberalism. What other critics have aptly labeled casino capitalism, fast capitalism, and vulture capitalism, David Harvey delineates and links to both planned political systems and the whole way of life of neoliberalism. His work is an impressive fusion of ideological and cultural critique.

As a cultural theorist trained in social sciences, Harvey relies heavily on data, statistics, and empirical case studies. Conversely, Hardt and Negri, humanists in the tradition of European philosophy like Agamben, compare and contrast the history of legal and political systems. They do Continental philosophy. Michaels for his part uses commonsensical yet innovative polemical argumentation in the tradition of American pragmatism. All these contemporary cultural critics are responding in their different ways to consequences of the passage from the Welfare State to the hegemony of neoliberal political economy. In the process, they revitalize the approaches of Marxist social science, Continental philosophy, and neopragmatism while reviving the mission of the public intellectual. Womack seeks to elude all such foreign methods by retribalizing, that is, reenergizing tribal traditions, perspectives, and land holdings treated as life-sustaining resources in a hostile white world. The Native American Renaissance entails homecoming and defensive sovereignty. At the same time it puts on poignant display the counter-globalization tendencies of minorities that are a central feature of twenty-first-century experience and theory. When all is said and done, subalterns can speak. They are part of the disorganized multitude.

In this context, the high-profile work of Alain Badiou is something of an outlier. On the one hand, he addresses the degraded life world of contemporary "unleashed capitalism." Like others, he dates this latest phase of capitalism from the counter-revolution of the 1970s and its symbolic culmination in the 2007 presidential election in France of Nicolas Sarkozy. Written for the general public and a bestseller in France, his spirited fast-paced *The Meaning of Sarkozy* (2007) paints in detail a grim picture of neoliberal times. On the other hand, this polemic, oddly enough, does not mention neoliberalism while all along closely paralleling the indictments of Hardt and Negri, Michaels, and Harvey. As a French political philosopher, Badiou is interested in the history of resistances to capitalism dating from the French Revolution to May 1968, the phases of which he specifies with care. But the Byzantine technical history of capitalist economics is neither his concern nor his specialty. What Badiou adds, nonetheless, to the catalogue of current neoliberal economic outrages are, for example, the systematic reductions of inheritance taxes that perpetuate hereditary wealth; the nonstop emphasis on selfish personal gain and savage competition; the "dictatorship of the market" (48) in all spheres of life including the arts; and the spread worldwide of walls and surveillance devices to lock out the poor, people of color, and foreigners. Along the way Badiou excoriates politicians and mainstream media for systematically serving the wealthy. And he is especially hard on leftist converts (socialists included) to the neoliberal dogma of the free market.

For Badiou the only viable solution to capitalism is communism. The world must "move beyond capitalism, private property, financial circulation, the despotic state ... " (39). This "communist hypothesis," as he propounds it here and elsewhere, is linked to the key performative maxim "there is only one world" (60), an existential as well as a political axiom. Badiou's argument raises the question of where things stand with contemporary identity politics. His straightforward answer: "The principle of the existence of a single world does not contradict the endless play of identities and differences" (68).

Critics of Badiou regularly single out certain features of his systematic philosophy, which comes to a culmination and much public attention during the opening years of the new century. The usual list includes complaints about his faith in universalist truths (most deriving from science and mathematics); his relentless advocacy of fidelity to a single cause or life-changing miraculous "event"; and his Platonist, seemingly aristocratic, contempt for current democracy in both its representative statist and its parliamentary party forms. He deplores the sham of voting, for instance. I concur with these criticisms of Badiou. In addition to his avoiding political economy, I find disappointing and perplexing the absence in Badiou of solutions to well-documented political problems. Of course, he fashions the communist argument as a "hypothesis" in order not to draw up programs. This way, he calculates, the future remains open to experimentation and innovation, with past missteps firmly in mind. In any event, in our time strong cases against capitalism must be made and communist options entertained. Badiou forwards this argument much more directly and incisively than all other major twenty-first-century theorists.

A key element of the renaissance of twenty-first-century theory involves mounting attention to the dramatic changes affecting the university under neoliberal conditions. Several dozen recent books explore this topic. Jeffrey Williams argues a new twenty-first-century subfield has matured that he usefully labels "critical university studies" (J. Williams 2012). The most dynamic branch of this subdiscipline dwells on academic labor studies. In my judgment the best book in the field is Marc Bousquet's *How the University Works: Higher Education and the Low-Wage Nation* (2008). From the vantage point of the twenty-first-century theory renaissance, this book and the new field revitalize both personal criticism and institutional critique by focusing on work, specifically disposable academic workers, offering macroscopic critical perspectives on the university. As I write, "corporate university" appears to be the most widely accepted critical term depicting today's neoliberalized higher education.[2] Here I offer a cameo of its American version for remaining skeptics.

Beginning in the 1970s, the corporate university in the US started transforming the teaching workforce from approximately 75% of the faculty tenured or on the tenure track to by the early twenty-first century about 75% contingent faculty and a mere 25% in the tenure stream. The American academic work force is roughly 1.5 million professors. This reversal constitutes a major transformation of the teaching corps toward precarity. Meanwhile the funding of the university gradually shifted the burden onto student tuitions, private gifts and endowments, plus auxiliary businesses ("profit centers") often outsourced such as campus food courts, bookstores, gift shops, parking, housing, and logo licensing and merchandising. US universities have come increasingly to prize patents, copyrights, and cooperative financial arrangements with corporations. Government support for public higher education has

---

[2]In a wide-ranging review essay, "The Post-Welfare State University," Jeffrey Williams assesses several dozen books on the history of the American university, outlining five different directions they follow. He uses the term "post-Welfare State university" to locate it historically, although common usage gravitates to "corporate university."

diminished dramatically in recent decades. It is not uncommon for a university's annual operating budget to have dropped from 50% to 15% state supported. And a substantial amount of this reduced funding comes from new state-run lotteries (casino capitalism). Undergraduate student debt has increased precipitously in tandem with steep tuition rises and loss of state funding. The majority of students have to work extended low-wage hours, which increases time to completion of degree, dropout rates, and debt.

In the era of the corporate university, education has been turned into a private rather than a social good. New unregulated and unaccredited, expensive for-profit higher education institutions continue to pop up everywhere. Given considerable oversupplies of PhDs in most fields, graduate students have for their part slowed time to degree. They fill the ranks of the contingent labor force as long-term teaching assistants while being pressured to publish and professionalize in order to compete in fierce job markets. Ten years in a PhD program has become typical. Half that time was the norm in the preceding decades (1945–1975). Graduate student debt has proliferated. In addition, faculty governance, its role in shared democratic decision-making, has eroded as many more layers of administration have been added and as top-down managerial practices borrowed from the corporate world have come to predominate (Ginsberg). Academic CEO pay has skyrocketed. Given such forces at play, the mission has shifted from enlightenment and critical citizenship education to vocational training and professional preparation. The public university today resembles Wal-Mart more than the ivory tower of earlier eras. Speaking in London during 2009, Italian philosopher Franco Berardi concluded, "In the first decade of the new century intellectual labor was made precarious and forced to accept any kind of economic blackmail. The criminal class enslaved the cognitive class: knowledge was fractilised, revenue reduced, exploitation and stress grew and grew."

Marc Bousquet highlights three waves of contemporary academic labor theory and practice in North America. The first wave from the 1960s and 1970s saw more than half the faculty unionized in state institutions. It was linked with the broader movement of the postwar Welfare State era toward public employee unions and workplace democracy. The second wave, coming to prominence during the Reagan era, witnessed the arrival of neoliberal market theory promoted by administrators, politicians, and business people. It remains committed to "assessment, ranking, pay-as-you-go, revenue maximization, and continuous competition in pursuit of excellence..." (93). It has facilitated the rise of the disposable academic workforce. Associated with graduate student unionization drives starting in the 1990s, the third wave propounds nonmarket or market regulation accounts of academic labor.

Bousquet identifies with the third wave in his project of critiquing the corporate university and its dominant job market ideology. He is particularly critical of the reigning supply-side model of the so-called job "market." He argues there is not an oversupply of PhDs but a deliberate undersupply of decent jobs. If higher education were to adopt a model of 85% tenure stream and 15% contingent labor, as recommended in 1993 by the American Association of University Professors, there would be a labor shortage and plenty of jobs (AAUP). Or if the wages of all contingent workers were fair—for example, $8,000–$10,000 per course instead of the usual $2,000–$3,000—there would no longer be an incentive to exploit academic workers. Another way to turn things around would be to unionize faculty (contingent and tenure stream), which Bousquet advocates while soberly assessing the past problems of academic unions. Part of Bousquet's mission is to convince not only faculty but also their influential professional organizations to abandon the rhetoric of second-wave neoliberal market theory in favor of third-wave discourse. Not incidentally, he, like Franco Berardi, correctly observes that the corporate university is a "global phenomenon" (176) increasingly common in Europe and the global South and enforced by conditionality agreements of support required by the IMF, WB, and most other funding agencies, governmental and non-governmental.

Marc Bousquet's engagé work on academic labor attracted early attention with a special issue of the journal *Works and Days* (2003) that ran a dozen articles in response to four of his essays (Derrickson). These essays later became parts of *How the University Works*. In his Afterword to that special issue, Bousquet calls for a project of "affective mapping" that links personal feelings to work conditions. He singles out among contingent faculty widespread feelings of desperation, betrayal, and anxiety. Indeed, his very scholarly book is shot through with anger, sarcasm, and outrage, a distinctive tone all his own of intimate critique.

To the criticism of Bousquet in the special issue of *Works and Days*, I add several points of my own. In his account of academic labor, Marc Bousquet gives very little time to the beleaguered tenured faculty in favor of super exploited contingent workers. Also he overlooks internal class tensions between and within the ranks of faculty, administrators, and students. However, he does pointedly criticize unions for agreeing to lower-paying tiers for younger members. His treatment of privatization is skimpy as is his discussion of debt. Bousquet has almost nothing, positive or negative, to say about minorities, affirmative action, or diversity programs. But what he forcefully advances for cultural theory is the project of teaching the university and most notably its exploitation of labor. The message of his passionate book is that there are fierce cultural struggles going on not just outside but also inside the university.

One of the readers of my manuscript suggested that I spell out the criteria I employ in selecting theory favorites. My favorites exhibit some combination of innovation, relevance, and influence. They tend to be passionate and critical, lucid and stylish, aimed at a general public. While they look back and historicize issues, they contribute to the future of the field, breaking new ground, especially in formulating or refurbishing useful concepts such as multitude, tribalcentrism, and bare life. And although some of these works are not the first, second, or third books on their topics, they are the best, meaning the most well-informed, trenchant, and critical. Examples include Harvey on neoliberalism and Bousquet on the corporate university. In addition, some of my theory favorites, for instance Michaels, are smart, that is, self-consciously and polemically excessive, original, and bold.

Alongside all these politically engaged works of cultural theory, there is a wide-ranging renaissance of academic literary theory in the twenty-first century, particularly responding to globalization. I would cite such contemporary literary types as Anglophone, Black Atlantic, Francophone, indigenous, InterAmerican, Pacific Basin, and Transatlantic literatures. All these literatures have come to undisputed scholarly recognition and flowering in the twenty-first century. In addition, the worldwide phenomenon of national political devolution has very recently revitalized minor language traditions and literatures. In the UK examples would include Irish, Scottish, and Welsh languages and literatures. In the US instances range from tribal to immigrant non-English "foreign" language literatures exemplified in the Shell and Sollors anthology. This transformation has dramatically broadened the scope and definition of national literatures. Other distinctive features of the renaissance in literary theory include, for example, Franco Moretti's collective project on the novel as a cyclical global form, new cognitive neurobiological theories of literature (Holland), and the rebarbarization of mainstream genres from below. In the latter case, for instance, slam, performance poetry, and hip hop have injected new oral and musical energies into the poetry world (Gioia, "Disappearing"). The revolutionary eruptions of minority literatures, first flaring in the late twentieth century, continue energetically across the globe into the new century. This includes most notably literatures by women, people of color, and LGBTQ writers, for example, in post-communist nations. Last but not least, born-digital electronic literature comes into initial prominence with the extensive online anthologies posted in 2006 and 2011 by the Electronic Literature Organization. The twenty-first century has witnessed upsurges of new theories, forms, and parameters of literature.

The renaissance in theory is, to be sure, not simply a matter of a handful of groundbreaking books and theories, my favorites or yours. As noted in earlier chapters, there are numerous backlashes as well as revivals underway such as formalist and phenomenological close reading. In its current state, poststructuralism is entering a new phase, and theory of postmodernism is coming back. In a retro theory wave, moreover, many publishers have recently been reprinting theory books from the 1970s, 1980s, and 1990s. For its part cultural studies, which the current chapter illustrates, has relaxed its longstanding commitment to national borders and traditions, taking into account more and more transnational global phenomena. Meanwhile, American studies has self-consciously fashioned a new globalized paradigm for the twenty-first century as demonstrated by the two dozen contributors to the landmark volume *The Futures of American Studies* (2002), edited and ably introduced by Donald Pease and Robyn Wiegman, leaders and architects of the reconfigured field. As my map indicates (Figure 1), there are numerous new fields of theory such as affective studies, ecocriticism, and cognitive studies. Other longstanding fields of criticism are undergoing revitalization, for instance, religion and literature, economics and literature, and narrative theory. Some theories like postcolonialism and New Historicism have by now spread so far and wide as to constitute the air most critics breathe. Segments of the twenty-first-century theory renaissance involve vigorous critical countercurrents such as the broad array of explicit antitheory sentiments gathered in *Theory's Empire* (2005) and sampled in Chapter 2. The rebirth of the public intellectual, which began during the cultural wars of the late 1980s and 1990s, continues apace in the new century. It has lost some of its novelty but none of its relevance particularly for universities. Over time the cultural wars have shifted critical focus from Great Books and curriculum to the corporate university's disposable labor and debilitating student debt.

How does the twenty-first-century theory renaissance relate to today's corporate university? The university is home to theory and its renaissance. Insofar as it encourages innovation, research, and publication, theory cooperates with the mission of the corporate university. In addition, theory contributes to the long-standing modern, though increasingly vestigial, university goals of promoting literacy, critical citizenship, and appreciation of the arts in the context of tradition. Much of contemporary theory is historicist and comparatist in orientation as is the university by tradition. Furthermore, theory aids and abets the ancient admonition to know thyself, although it characteristically extends the project of reflection beyond self to society.

Yet because it came to prominence during the decades when the corporate university began replacing the Welfare State university, theory has developed in a milieu shaped by labor agitation and MBA-style administrative managerialism as well as by earlier minority activism. It has often found itself critical of the university. From the outset in the 1970s such struggles involved advocating antinomian programs in women's studies and gender studies plus race and ethnicity studies; challenging tradition by establishing multicultural curricula and diversity in admissions and hiring; and unionizing of faculty and teaching assistants to insure adequate pay, benefits, and democratic input. More recently, theory has defended the university during the culture wars while also criticizing it for the practices of increasing tuition and student debt; deprofessionalizing the faculty into a majority low-wage workforce; and diminishing the sphere of democratic shared decision making. So the relation that theory has to today's corporate university is at once supportive and critical but increasingly so.

I can imagine a day when many more university administrators and external stakeholders decide to relax or perhaps renounce traditions of academic freedom and shared governance, discouraging or silencing all manner of socially critical theory. In such a scenario, I wonder if theorists, many or a few, might decide to depart through silence, careerism, internal exile, or physical leave taking. It's difficult to imagine any long-term benefits for the partners in such scenarios. They would create more disenchanted adversaries inside and outside the university; more openings for yet higher percentages of alienated low-wage faculty; and more vanquished antagonists. But in my view, theorists and the university are stuck with each other for the foreseeable future. Historically speaking, it has not always been thus. Theory thrived in many times and places separate from the academy. No doubt, the ongoing corporatization of the university will exacerbate relations, generating more calls for unionization, more demoralized internal constituents, and more energetic entrepreneurial projects and debts. Just as students are positioned as consumers, and as knowledge and wisdom have morphed into content-information-product, professors have become individual entrepreneurs in search of support for innovative and profitable outcomes. So, no matter whether professors are dedicated to cultural critique, or to formalist aesthetics, or to pure science, these entrepreneurs are caught up in the flood of values and idols swirling around and through the corporate university. As matters stand now, theory has a role as both support and, increasingly, critic of the corporate university.

10
Theory futures

I want to make a claim, a prediction, directed at aspiring theorists and all other interested parties. Consider this my letter to young colleagues. The future for theory in higher education, specifically in the humanities and social sciences, looks good. To use the dominant laissez-faire market language of the day, I am bullish. This is with the longish as well as the middle and short terms in mind. Of course, there are some caveats and complications. But I am offering a buy signal. And you readers, especially theorists, may well wonder why.

For starters, the demand for research and publication in higher education is not going away anytime soon. On the contrary, it continues to seep out from major research universities into many other educational institutions. This has been going on particularly in North America since the 1960s and has spread across the globe. Within many humanities and social science disciplines, theory answers the call. It provides new topics of inquiry, new approaches, and new objects for investigation. Here I would cite the continuous productivity, for example, of Marxist, poststructuralist, and postcolonial theory; of feminist, gender, and queer theory; and particularly of the many innovative subdisciplines charted at the outset of this book in Figure 1. Mix and match any three or more of those items to create a new area of inquiry. Antitheory and posttheory sentiments of recent decades only make sense in the context of theory as a dominant paradigm. Inside higher education theory appears an empire to some of its strongest opponents. Well, amen, despite the inept metaphor and associated hysteria.

Large numbers of undergraduate and graduate students are required to take one or more courses of introductory theory, contemporary or classical. In addition, there are usually optional courses beyond these. Various institutions offer minors, certificates, and specializations in theory. There are numerous guides, dictionaries, glossaries, and anthologies covering theory. And their numbers keep increasing. All of this is what I think of as Theory Incorporated.

In recent years I, like others, have been invited as a theorist to lecture and teach in foreign countries: Brazil, China, Egypt, Estonia, Finland, Germany, and Hungary in my case. The textbook I worked on, *Norton Anthology of Theory and Criticism*, makes nearly half of its annual sales outside the United States. Theory has gone global. It may be expected to continue going global, furthermore, by incorporating "foreign" elements, both classic and contemporary. At present, theory in North America and Europe does not usually include Arabic, Chinese, Indian, Japanese, Persian, or other non-European traditions. In the future, it will increasingly do so. During its initial stages, America will likely be the hub of the emerging world republic of theory (Keucheyan 255).

In a nutshell, the way I see it, theory provides many resources: cultural capital, fertile canons and traditions, critique, useful tools, a professional lingua franca, plus ample materials and new perspectives for research, publication, and teaching. This has motivated innumerable franchising operations, part of Theory Incorporated.

Now if aspiring theorists ask me which theory in particular to invest in today, we have to face some complications. Up until the mid-1990s, contemporary theory, for example in literary studies, was configured as a set of schools and movements, both major and minor. This picture, of course, changes with different academic disciplines and departments. In North American literary studies and English departments in particular, the sequence of contemporary theories covers, to recite the standard list one last time, Marxism, psychoanalysis, formalism, myth criticism, existentialism and phenomenology, hermeneutics and reader-response theory, structuralism, poststructuralism, feminism, race and ethnicity theory, New Historicism, gender and queer theory, postcolonial theory, personal criticism, and cultural studies. Despite this abundance, the dominant forces over these years were during the 1950s and 1960s formalism, the 1970s and 1980s poststructuralism, and the 1990s to the present cultural studies. Coherence can be found amid expanding plenty.

Starting in the 1970s, however, crossovers and fusions, postmodern pastiches and assemblages, began to appear. I would cite again as an instance the well-known pioneering Marxist feminist deconstructive postcolonial work of Gayatri Spivak. Many other examples of theoretical eclecticism could be listed. Since the early 1990s, North American cultural studies has rather quickly branched out from its more or less coherent British forerunner into dozens of semiautonomous subfields or studies areas. I have in mind whiteness studies, body studies, trauma studies, border studies, disability studies, animal studies, subaltern studies, working-class studies, and so on. Each of these areas has its own history and theoretical configuration. None is in a position of dominance, quite the contrary. So the theory renaissance has a structure of disaggregation. Not surprisingly, my argument is that twenty-first-century theory is unmasterable yet knowable. It remains roughly recognizable in its current disseminated highly productive postmodern form as "theory."

Like any investment or purchase today, this one that we are entertaining—to buy into theory and in which one or ones—faces a proliferation of choices. We all regularly confront this type of problem whether we are looking to buy a breakfast cereal, a six pack of beer, or a bottle of wine. Innumerable choices confront us accompanied frequently by muted feelings of bewilderment, dismay, astonishment. Not unexpectedly, I have had doctoral students ask me whether to buy, sell, or hold theory and cultural studies and in just these terms. The structure of our late capitalist consumer societies consists precisely of abundance and disorganization typified as gaudy dispersion. Neither higher education nor theory has escaped this form. In any case, I'm sending a general buy signal.

Everywhere there are guides, top ten lists, books for dummies, and self-help manuals and media. If you are recognized today as a professional theorist or a serious devotee of theory, you are unashamedly positioned from time to time as an investment counselor, a futures advisor. That's the role I play here. People want very badly to know what are the newest approaches to the arts, society, and culture. What is the latest thing? In these times, such market vanguardism is insistent. Given this context, theory gets swept up in fashion. There is a queer theory approach, a postcolonial approach, and many hot cultural studies approaches.

Some areas or niches are very hot and some not. This is part of what I think of as the Theory Market. We live in a world of commodities, abundance, advertising, competition, speeded-up obsolescence, utilitarian choices, and calculated investments. It is no surprise that theory as well as scholarship, research, and academic publishing reside there. This goes for the arts and humanities as well as the sciences, social sciences, and professions.

But there is a further complication. Can one choose, for example, feminism, critical race theory, or postcolonial theory as an attractive option preferable to others? These theories stem from certain personal as well as collective experiences, histories, oppressions, values. In this sense theory is rooted in standpoints, worldviews, and existential situations. The category "consumer choice"—construed as an individual human right and citizen's responsibility, according to today's neoliberal theory of homo economicus—doesn't begin to explain how one comes to such theory.

A great deal of what counts as theory has a critical edge and cuts across the grain of contemporary society. The tools of the trade today bear me out: Marxist-derived ideological analysis, race-class-gender cultural critique, deconstruction of venerable binary concepts, minority counter-histories, psychoanalytically inflected hermeneutics of suspicion, rhetorical analysis of political discourse, Foucaultian genealogy, and so on. This equipment is part of the DNA of many contemporary humanistic and social scientific fields. It complements the usual and expected traditional street smarts, self-reflection, and methodological prudence plus close reading and exegesis. If we look around, much criticism needs to be done. Theory is well positioned and predisposed to do it. This is why, in considerable part, conservative cultural warriors condemn it. They have kept on the attack for decades. Theory represents continuous challenge. That to me provides ample reason to recommend as well as defend it.

The situation today of newly minted PhD theory specialists seeking work in, for example, North American higher education differs tellingly from that of the high watermark during the 1980s. In the eighties, theory broke away from its long-standing subordinate role and became a free-standing specialty and major paradigm for various disciplines, certainly literary studies. Nowadays, theory has permeated most of the specialties and subspecialties of various disciplines to the point that everyone, it seems, is doing theory of some sort. That includes for literature the local Shakespearean, Victorianist, and ethnic specialist. Like feminism, theory is everywhere and nowhere. So there is no apparent need to hire any theory specialist per se. Today's applied theory has innumerable local habitations and names. Consequently, stand-alone theory has fallen by the wayside. It is not a preferred academic specialty, but a secondary backup one, playing supporting roles.

Beginning card-carrying theorists, therefore, need a professional identity linked to a more venerable specialty or recognized subspecialty, not this recent upstart field alone. To give a few examples, British Romantic celebrity literary culture, or globalization in Renaissance travel literature, or early Cold War American confessional poetry would nicely complement and moderate primary investment in theory. Here, and everywhere else across the literature curriculum, well-attested historical periods, genres, and themes reassert the mid-century structure of the discipline. It is not that theory is dead now. Not at all. It is ubiquitous and thriving, but quite abruptly in the back seat and in the old vehicle. The modern university lives on in many of its structures.

The various reconfigurations of theory charted thus far are tied to the postmodernization of higher education. It is a matter of uneven development. On the one hand, the university is a modernist institution in which early twentieth-century disciplines and departments constitute its perdurable infrastructure and its very architecture. On the other hand, these modern disciplines have lost their autonomy in a new era of interdisciplinarity and crossdisciplinarity. Think of all the new fields built up following the 1960s such as gender studies, ethnic studies, semiotics, or cultural studies and dozens of more recent subdisciplines like cognitive studies, disability studies, and globalization studies. I have not even mentioned all the new fields in the sciences.

But where are the new "interdisciplines" housed? Rarely in their own departments, rather in skimpily funded and casually staffed programs or centers. This is one of my pet peeves. Are there teaching jobs in these exciting and productive fields? Well, no, not exactly, not directly. They usually have to be camouflaged to fit into the accredited modern (prepostmodern) disciplines and specialties. If, for example, you are an English professor interested in punk—punk music, dress, dancing, and cultural locations—you need to find a literary tie-in such as punk slang, lyrics, and zines. You position yourself as specializing in late twentieth-century literature and culture, with a focus on subcultural vernacular aesthetic discourses. Not surprisingly, many jobs seekers in this phase of theory and interdisciplinarity are in disguise. On one hand, the university, its departmentalization and staffing, appear frozen in an earlier mid-twentieth-century configuration. On the other, offshoots and crossovers proliferate like crabgrass. Theory is part of this growth and deterritorialization. It went viral in the fin de siècle and continues to do so in our new century. It's a prolific renaissance accompanied by countercurrents.

Here is what I or probably any veteran theorist would say nowadays to a PhD student aspiring to be an academic theorist. Invest in theory. Just be aware that cosmetic finessing will be required to your professional image and curriculum vitae. Makeovers are necessary. Flexibility is the watchword. Have a traditional profile, fit in the old framework, and be instantly recognizable to the oldest of old timers. Yet appear innovative, creative, smart, committed to the new, even to the newest of the new, but again within the old frame of recognized disciplines and specialties. Face the fact, for instance in North America, that less than half of new PhDs will secure a tenure-track job after an average of ten years of PhD study and tens of thousands of dollars in student debt. Moreover, part of your makeover routine is to look suitable as well for the insecure Macjobs that in the twenty-first-century US constitute about three-quarters of the higher education academic workforce. Be aware that this degraded job category calls for trimming back obvious theory inclinations in favor of robust basic education. Welcome to the corporate university.

At this point I want to own up to a fantasy of mine. Sometimes I feel theory should be part of basic education like composition and mathematics. In this scenario there ought to be a course or two of interdisciplinary theory required of all undergraduate students. It would doubtlessly be staffed by faculty in the humanities and social sciences, consisting of core and optional modules, drawing from contemporary and perhaps classic sources. But then I vacillate, thinking theory should be reserved for certain majors and only in the advanced upper-division course work. In the former scenario, theory is tantamount to critical thinking in its various genuine contemporary modes. In the latter, theory is advanced critical and creative thinking as well as methods and approaches within the delimited contexts of recognized disciplines and their traditions. A great deal is in question here: the places of critical and creative thinking in higher education curriculum; the future of Theory Incorporated and the Theory Market, including the theory job market for PhDs; and the mission of higher education in today's societies.

What lies in the immediate future for theory? Here are three predictions. To begin with, theory will continue to be disseminated through innumerable specialties, periods, subspecialties, disciplines, and national contexts to the point of losing its identity in various settings. So be it. At the same time, challenges can be expected in North America and elsewhere to the now standard three graduate and undergraduate theory course offerings and requirements, namely Introduction to Theory, History of Theory, and Modern/Contemporary Theory. Let theorists be prepared to defend while continuously transforming their bread-and-butter courses. Lastly, theory must go global. To reiterate, it needs to include materials from Arabic, Chinese, Indian, Japanese, Persian, and other traditions, reaching back often to ancient times and recontextualizing theory's lingering Eurocentrism. Such globalizing will not bring an end to national identities, regional affiliations, or local distinctions, quite the opposite.

There are those who say theory is past. They generally mean poststructuralism or the broader interdisciplinary configuration of theory in the 1980s and 1990s. They are right, yet only superficially as I have argued throughout this book. Theory in the sense of methods and approaches, perennial texts and intellectual problems, plus critique is alive and well. It is indispensable for those in humanistic and social scientific fields, students as well as faculty. It shapes professional discourse, consciously and unconsciously. What is past and missing just now is the general sense of excitement sometimes approaching hysteria that accompanied the early days of the theory boom during the 1980s. The current stage of market society, casino capitalism, solicits quick fashion changes, rapid obsolescence, and hyper excitement, both manufactured and real. Theory is caught up in these shifting currents of highs and lows.

BIBLIOGRAPHY

Abrams, M. H. *Natural Supernaturalism: Tradition and Revolution in Romantic Literature*. New York: W. W. Norton, 1971. Print.

Adorno, Theodor W. "Cultural Criticism and Society." In *Prisms*. Eds. Samuel Weber and Shierry Weber. London: Spearman, 1967. 19–34. Print.

Agamben, Giorgio. *Homo Sacer: Sovereign Power and Bare Life*. Trans. Daniel Heller-Roazen. Stanford, CA: Stanford University Press, 1998. Print.

Althusser, Louis. "Ideology and Ideological State Apparatuses." In *Lenin and Philosophy and Other Essays*. Trans. Ben Brewster. New York: Monthly Review Press, 1971. 127–186. Print.

American Association of University Professors Committee G. "Report: On the Status of Non-Tenure-Track Faculty." *Academe* 78.6 (1992): 39–48. Print.

Anderson, Amanda. *The Way We Argue Now: A Study in the Cultures of Theory*. Princeton, NJ: Princeton University Press, 2006. Print.

Armstrong, Paul B. *How Literature Plays with the Brain: The Neuroscience of Reading and Art*. Baltimore, MD: Johns Hopkins University Press, 2013. Print.

Aronowitz, Stanley. "The Last Good Job in America." In *Chalk Lines: The Politics of Work in the Managed University*. Ed. Randy Martin. Durham, NC: Duke University Press, 1998. 202–222. Print.

Auerbach, Erich. "Odysses' Scar." In *Mimesis: The Representation of Reality in Western Literature*. Trans. Willard R. Trask. Princeton, NJ: Princeton University Press, 1953. 3–23. Print.

Badiou, Alain. *The Meaning of Sarkozy*. Trans. David Fernbach. London: Verso, 2008. Print.

Balakrishnan, Gopal, Ed. *Debating EMPIRE*. New York: Verso, 2003. Print.

Baron, Naomi S. "Redefining Reading: The Impact of Digital Communication Media." *PMLA* 128.1 (2013): 193–200. Print.

Barthes, Roland. *S/Z: An Essay*. Trans. Richard Miller. New York: Hill and Wang, 1974. Print.

Bartolovich, Crystal. "Humanities of Scale: Marxism, Surface Reading—and Milton." *PMLA* 127.1 (2012): 115–121. Print.

Bauerlein, Mark. "Social Constructionism: Philosophy for the Academic Workplace." *Partisan Review* 68.2 (2001): 228–241. Print.

Belsey, Catherine. *A Future for Criticism*. Oxford: Wiley-Blackwell, 2011. Print.

Berardi, Franco. "Communism Is Back but We Should Call It the Therapy of Singularisation (February 2009)." Available at: http://www. generation-online.org/p/fp_bifo6.htm [accessed December 20, 2013].

Bérubé, Michael. *The Left at War*. New York: New York University Press, 2009. Print.

Best, Stephen and Sharon Marcus, Eds. "Surface Reading: An Introduction." *Representations* 108. Fall (2009): 1–21. Special issue on "The Way We Read Now." Print.

Bewes, Timothy. "Reading with the Grain: A New World in Literary Criticism." *Differences: A Journal of Feminist Cultural Studies* 21.3 (2010): 1–33. Print.

Bleich, David. *Subjective Criticism*. Baltimore, MD: Johns Hopkins University Press, 1981. Print.

Bloom, Harold. *The Anxiety of Influence: A Theory of Poetry*. New York: Oxford University Press, 1973. Print.

Boltanski, Luc. *On Critique: A Sociology of Emancipation*. Trans. Gregory Elliott. Cambridge: Polity, 2011. Print.

Bóron, Atilio A. *Empire and Imperialism: A Critical Reading of Michael Hardt and Antonio Negri*. London: Zed, 2005. Print.

Borràs, Laura, et al., Eds. *Electronic Literature Collection*. vol. 2 (2011). Available at: http://collection.eliterature.org/2/ [accessed June 29, 2013].

Bourdieu, Pierre. *Acts of Resistance: Against the Tyranny of the Market*. Trans. Richard Nice. New York: Free Press, 1999. Print.

Bousquet, Marc. *How the University Works: Higher Education and the Low-Wage Nation*. New York: New York University Press, 2008. Print.

Bradford, Richard W., Ed. *Teaching Theory*. London: Palgrave Macmillan, 2011. Print.

Brennan, Timothy. *Wars of Position: The Cultural Politics of Left and Right*. New York: Columbia University Press, 2006. Print.

Brooks, Cleanth. "The Language of Paradox." In *The Well Wrought Urn: Studies in the Structure of Poetry*. New York: Harcourt Brace, 1947. 3–21. Print.

Burke, Kenneth. *The Philosophy of Literary Form: Studies in Symbolic Action*. 3rd ed. Berkeley: University of California Press, 1973. Print.

Butler, Judith. "What is Critique? An Essay on Foucault's Virtue." In *The Political*. Ed. David Ingram. Malden, MA: Blackwell, 2002. 212–226. Print.

Caws, Mary Ann, Ed. *Textual Analysis: Some Readers Reading.* New York: MLA, 1986. Print.

Culler, Jonathan. *Literary Theory: A Very Short Introduction.* 2nd ed. New York: Oxford University Press, 2011. Print.

Cusset, François. *French Theory: How Foucault, Derrida, Deleuze, and Co. Transformed the Intellectual Life of the United States.* Trans. Jeff Fort with Josephine Berganza and Marlon Jones. Minneapolis: University of Minnesota Press, 2008. Print.

Davis, Colin. *Critical Excess: Overreading in Derrida, Deleuze, Levinas, Žižek, and Cavell.* Stanford, CA: Stanford University Press, 2010. Print.

De Man, Paul. *Allegories of Reading: Figural Language in Rousseau, Nietzsche, Rilke, and Proust.* New Haven, CT: Yale University Press, 1979. Print.

Derrickson, Teresa, Ed. "Information University: Rise of the Education Management Organization." *Works and Days* 21.1–2 (2003): 7–369. Special Issue on Marc Bousquet. Print.

Derrida Seminar Translation Project. Available at: derridaseminars.org [accessed September 13, 2013].

Derrida, Jacques. "Plato's Pharmacy." In *Dissemination.* Trans. Barbara Johnson. Chicago: University of Chicago Press, 1983. 61–171. Print.

———. *Specters of Marx: The State of Debt, The Work of Mourning, and the New Internationale.* Trans. Peggy Kamuf. New York: Routledge, 1994. Print.

———. "Autoimmunity: Real and Symbolic Suicides—A Dialogue with Jacques Derrida." In *Philosophy in a Time of Terror: Dialogues with Jürgen Habermas and Jacques Derrida.* Ed. Giovanna Borradori. Chicago: University of Chicago Press, 2003. 85–136, 186–193. Print.

———. "*Circonfession*" *lu par l'auteur.* La Bibliotheque des Voix Series. Paris: Des Femmes, 2006. 5 CDs.

———. *Séminaire La bête et le souverain, Volume II (2002–2003).* Eds. Michel Lisse, Marie-Louise Mallet, and Ginette Michaud. Paris: Éditions Galilée, 2010. Print.

Derrida, Jacques and Elisabeth Roudinesco. "Violence Against Animals." In *For What Tomorrow... A Dialogue.* Trans. Jeff Fort. Stanford, CA: Stanford University Press, 2004. 62–76. Print.

Derrida, dir. Kirby Dick and Amy Ziering Kofman. Jane Doe Films. 2002. DVD, Zeitgeist Video, 2003.

Di Leo, Jeffrey, et al., Eds. *Neoliberalism, Education, Terrorism: Contemporary Dialogues.* Boulder, CO: Paradigm, 2013. Print.

During, Simon, Ed. *The Cultural Studies Reader.* 3rd ed. New York: Routledge, 2007. Print.

Eagleton, Terry. *After Theory*. New York: Basic, 2003. Print.
———. *Ideology: An Introduction*. 2nd ed. London: Verso, 2007. Print.
Ebert, Teresa. *The Task of Cultural Critique*. Urbana: University of Illinois Press, 2009. Print.
Eco, Umberto. *Travels in Hyperreality*. Trans. William Weaver. Orlando, FL: Harcourt, Brace, 1986. Print.
Edmundson, Mark. "Against Readings." *Profession* (2009): 56–65. Print.
Eliot, Jane and Derek Attridge, Eds. *Theory after "Theory."* Manifesto Series. New York: Routledge, 2011. Print.
Ellis, John M. *Literature Lost: Social Agendas and the Corruption of the Humanities*. New Haven, CT: Yale University Press, 1997. Print.
Felski, Rita. "After Suspicion." *Profession* (2009): 28–35. Print.
Florida, Richard. *The Rise of the Creative Class: And How It's Transforming Work, Leisure, Community, and Everyday Life*. New York: Basic, 2002. Print.
Foucault, Michel. "What is Critique?" In *The Political*. Ed. David Ingram. Malden, MA: Blackwell, 2002. 191–211. Print.
Franklin, Cynthia G. *Academic Lives: Memoir, Cultural Theory, and the University Today*. Athens, GA: University of Georgia Press, 2009. Print.
Fraser, Nancy and Axel Honneth. *Redistribution or Recognition? A Political-Philosophical Exchange*. Trans. Joel Golb, James Ingram, and Christine Wilke. New York: Verso, 2003. Print.
Freedman, Diana P., Olivia Frey, and Frances Murphy Zauhar, Eds. *The Intimate Critique: Autobiographical Literary Criticism*. Durham, NC: Duke University Press, 1993. Print.
Gallop, Jane. "The Historicization of Literary Studies and the Fate of Close Reading." *Profession* (2007): 181–186. Print.
———. "Close Reading in 2009." *Association of Departments of English Bulletin* 149 (2010): 15–19. Print.
Ginsberg, Benjamin. *The Fall of the Faculty: The Rise of the All-Administrative University and Why It Matters*. New York: Oxford University Press, 2011. Print.
Gioia, Dana. *Can Poetry Matter? Essays on Poetry and American Culture*. Tenth Anniversary ed. Saint Paul, MN: Graywolf Press, 2002. Print.
———. "Disappearing Ink: Poetry at the End of Print Culture." In *Disappearing Ink: Poetry at the End of Print Culture*. Saint Paul, MN: Graywolf Press, 2004. 3–31. Print.
Goodheart, Eugene. *Does Literary Studies Have a Future*. Madison: University of Wisconsin Press, 1999. Print.
———. "Criticism in the Age of Discourse." *Clio* 32.2 (2003): 205–208. Print.

Graff, Gerald. "Advocacy in the Classroom—Or the Curriculum? A Response." In *Advocacy in the Classroom: Problems and Possibilities*. Ed. Patricia Meyer Spacks. New York: St. Martin's Press, 1996. 425–431. Print.

Greene, Roland, et al., Eds. *The Princeton Encyclopedia of Poetry and Poetics*. 4th ed. Princeton, NJ: Princeton University Press, 2012. Print.

Groden, Michael, Martin Kreiswirth, and Imre Szeman, Eds. *Contemporary Literary and Cultural Theory: The Johns Hopkins Guide*. Baltimore, MD: Johns Hopkins University Press, 2012. Print.

Hall, Stuart and Martin Jacques, Eds. *New Times: The Changing Face of Politics in the 1990s*. London: Verso, 1990. Print.

Haraway, Donna. *Simians, Cyborgs, and Women: The Reinvention of Nature*. New York: Routledge, 1991. Print.

Hardt, Michael. "The Militancy of Theory." *South Atlantic Quarterly* 110.1 (Winter) (2011): 19–35. Print.

—— and Antonio Negri. *Empire*. Cambridge: Harvard University Press, 2000. Print.

Harvey, David. *The Condition of Postmodernity*. Cambridge, MA: Blackwell, 1990. Print.

——. *A Brief History of Neoliberalism*. New York: Oxford University Press, 2005. Print.

Hassan, Ihab. "Beyond Postmodernism." In *Quest of Nothing: Selected Essays*. Ed. Klaus Stierstofer. New York: AMS Press, 2010. 127–139. Print.

Hayles, N. Katherine, et al., Eds. *Electronic Literature Collection*. vol. 1 (2006). Available at: http://collection.eliterature.org/1/ [accessed June 29, 2012].

Hebdige, Dick. *Subculture: The Meaning of Style*. London: Routledge, 1979. Print.

Heidegger, Martin. "Language." In *Poetry, Language, Thought*. Trans. Albert Hofstadter. New York: Harper, 1975. 185–208. Print.

——. *The Fundamental Concepts of Metaphysics: World, Finitude, Solitude*. Trans. William McNeill and Nicholas Walker. Bloomington, IN: Indiana University Press, 1995. Print.

Holbo, John, Ed. *Framing Theory's Empire*. West Lafayette, IN: Parlor Press, 2007. Print.

Holland, Norman. "References." *Literature and the Brain*. Gainesville, FL: PsyArt Foundation, 2009. 409–443. Print.

hooks, bell. *Outlaw Culture: Resisting Representations*. New York: Routledge, 1994. Print.

Hoover, Paul, Ed. *Postmodern American Poetry: A Norton Anthology*, 2nd ed. New York: W. W. Norton, 2013. Print.

Horowitz, David. *The Professors: The 101 Most Dangerous Academics in America*. Washington, DC: Regnery, 2006. Print.

Hutcheon, Linda. "Gone Forever, But Here to Stay: The Legacy of the Postmodern." In *Postmodernism. What Moment?* Ed. Pelagia Goulimari. Manchester: Manchester University Press, 2007. 16–18. Print.

———, et al. "Postmodernism." In *The Princeton Encyclopedia of Poetry and Poetics*. 4th ed. Eds. Roland Greene, et al. Princeton, NJ: Princeton University Press, 2012. 1095–1097. Print.

Jacobs, Alan. *The Pleasures of Reading in an Age of Distraction*. New York: Oxford University Press, 2011. Print.

Jakobson, Roman and Claude Lévi-Strauss. "Charles Baudelaire's 'Les Chats'." In *The Structuralists: From Marx to Lévi-Strauss*. Eds. Richard T. and Fernande M. De George. Garden City: Doubleday, 1972. 124–146. Print.

Jameson, Fredric. *The Prison-House of Language: A Critical Account of Structuralism and Russian Formalism*. Princeton, NJ: Princeton University Press, 1972. Print.

———. *Postmodernism, or the Cultural Logic of Late Capitalism*. Durham, NC: Duke University Press, 1991. Print.

Jencks, Charles. *The Story of Post-Modernism: Five Decades of the Ironic, Iconic and Critical in Architecture*. Chichester: Wiley, 2011. Print.

Jenkins, Henry. *Textual Poachers: Television Fans and Participatory Culture*. New York: Routledge, 1992. Print.

———. *Convergence Culture: Where Old and New Media Collide*. New York: New York University Press, 2006. Print.

Johnson, Benjamin, Patrick Kavanagh and Kevin Mattson, Eds. *Steal This University: The Rise of the Corporate University and the Academic Labor Movement*. New York: Routledge, 2003. Print.

Juhasz, Alexandra. "A Truly New Genre." In *Inside Higher Ed*. May 3, 2011. Web. May 5, 2011.

Kelly, Michael, Ed. *Encyclopedia of Aesthetics*. 4 Vols. New York: Oxford University Press, 1998. Print.

Keucheyan, Razmig. *Left Hemisphere: Mapping Critical Theory Today*. New York: Verso, 2013. Print.

Khalip, Jacques, Ed. "Future Foucault." *South Atlantic Quarterly* 111.3 (2012), Special Issue. Print.

Knellwolf, Christa and Christopher Norris, Eds. *The Cambridge History of Literary Criticism*. Vol. IX: *Twentieth-Century Historical, Philosophical and Psychological Perspectives*. New York: Cambridge University Press, 2001. Print.

Lacan, Jacques. *Écrits: The First Complete Edition in English*. Trans. Bruce Fink, et al. New York: W. W. Norton, 2006. Print.

Laclau, Ernesto and Chantal Mouffe. *Hegemony and Socialist Strategy: Toward a Radical Democratic Politics*. London: Verso, 1985. Print.

Latour, Bruno. "Why Has Critique Run Out of Steam?" *Critical Inquiry* 30.2 (2004): 225–248. Print.

Leitch, Vincent B. "Taboo and Critique: Literary Criticism and Ethics."
    Association of Departments of English Bulletin 90. Fall (1988): 46–52.
    Print.
———. *Cultural Criticism, Literary Theory, Poststructuralism.* New York:
    Columbia University Press, 1992. Print.
———. *Postmodernism—Local Effects, Global Flows.* Series in
    Postmodern Culture. Albany: State University of New York Press,
    1996. Print.
———. *Theory Matters.* New York: Routledge, 2003. Print.
———. "Applied Theory." In *Living with Theory.* Manifesto Series.
    Oxford: Blackwell, 2008. 32–48. Print.
———. *American Literary Criticism Since the 1930s.* 2nd ed. New York:
    Routledge, 2010. Print.
———. Gen. Ed., et al. *Norton Anthology of Theory and Criticism.*
    2nd ed. 2010. New York: W. W. Norton, 2001. Print.
Lentricchia, Frank and Andrew DuBois, Eds. *Close Reading: The Reader.*
    Durham, NC: Duke University Press, 2003.
Machor, James L. and Philip Goldstein, Eds. *Reception Study: From
    Literary Theory to Cultural Studies.* New York: Routledge, 2001. Print.
McQuillan, Martin, et al., Eds. *Post-theory: New Directions in Criticism.*
    Edinburgh: Edinburgh University Press, 1999. Print.
Michaels, Walter Benn. *The Trouble with Diversity: How We Learned to
    Love Identity and Ignore Inequality.* New York: Henry Holt, 2006. Print.
Miller, J. Hillis. "Tradition and Difference." *Diacritics* 2.4 (Winter)
    (1972): 6–13. Print.
———. "Presidential Address 1986: The Triumph of Theory, the
    Resistance to Reading, and the Question of the Material Base." *PMLA*
    102.3 (1987): 281–291. Print.
Mitchell, W. J. T. and Arnold I. Davidson, Eds. *The Late Derrida.* Chicago:
    University of Chicago Press, 2007. Print.
Moraru, Christian. *Cosmodernism: American Narrative, Late
    Globalization, and the New Cultural Imaginary.* Ann Arbor: University
    of Michigan Press, 2011. Print.
———. Ed. "Focus on Metamodernism." *American Book Review* 34.4
    (2013): 3–15.
Moretti, Franco. *Graphs, Maps, Trees: Abstract Models for a Literary
    History.* London: Verso, 2005. Print.
———, Ed. *The Novel.* vol. 1: *History, Geography, and Culture*; vol. 2:
    Forms and Themes. Princeton, NJ: Princeton University Press, 2007.
    Print.
———. *Distant Reading.* London: Verso, 2013. Print.
National Endowment for the Arts. *Reading on the Rise: A New Chapter
    in American Literacy.* Research Brochure #03B. Washington, DC:
    NEA, Jan. 2009. Web. July 2, 2013.

Native Critics Collective. *Reasoning Together*. Norman: University of
    Oklahoma Press, 2008. Print.
Nealon, Jeffrey T. *Post-Postmodernism or, The Cultural Logic of Just-in-
    Time Capitalism*. Stanford, CA: Stanford University Press, 2012. Print.
Negri, Antonio. *Reflections on Empire*. Trans. Ed Emery. 2003;
    Cambridge: Polity Press, 2008. Print. [Three of thirteen chapters are
    coauthored by Michael Hardt.]
Newfield, Christopher. *Unmaking the Public University: The Forty-Year
    Assault on the Middle Class*. Cambridge: Harvard University Press,
    2008. Print.
Passavant, Paul and Jodi Dean, Eds. *Empire's New Clothes: Reading
    Hardt and Negri*. New York: Routledge, 2004. Print.
Patai, Daphne and Will H. Corral, Eds. *Theory's Empire: An Anthology of
    Dissent*. New York: Columbia University Press, 2005. Print.
Pease, Donald E. and Robyn Wiegman. "Futures." In *The Future of
    American Studies*. Eds. Donald E. Pease and Robyn Wiegman.
    Durham, NC: Duke University Press, 2002. 1–42. Print.
Peeters, Benoît. *Derrida*. Grandes Biographies Series. Paris: Flammarion,
    2010. Print.
———. *Trois ans avec Derrida: Les Carnets d'un biographe*. Paris:
    Flammarion, 2010.
Pratt, Mary Louise. "Interpretive Strategies/Strategic Interpretations: On
    Anglo-American Reader-Response Criticism." *Boundary 2* 11. Fall/
    Winter (1982–1983): 201–231. Print.
Pulitano, Elvira. *Toward a Native American Critical Theory*. Lincoln:
    University of Nebraska Press, 2003. Print.
Rabaté, Jean-Michel. *The Future of Theory*. Malden, MA: Blackwell,
    2002. Print.
Radway, Janice. *Reading the Romance: Women, Patriarchy, and Popular
    Literature*. Chapel Hill: University of North Carolina Press, 1991. Print.
Rancière, Jacques. "The Misadventures of Critical Thought." In *The
    Emancipated Spectator*. Trans. Gregory Elliott. London: Verso, 2011.
    25–49. Print.
Reger, Jo. *Everywhere and Nowhere: Contemporary Feminism in the
    United States*. NewYork: Oxford University Press, 2012. Print.
Ricoeur, Paul. *Freud and Philosophy: An Essay on Interpretation*. Trans.
    Denis Savage. The Terry Lectures. New Haven, CT: Yale University
    Press, 1970. Print.
Ryan, Michael, Gen. Ed., et al. *The Encyclopedia of Literary and Cultural
    Theory*. 3 Vols. Malden, MA: Wiley-Blackwell, 2011. Print.
Said, Edward W. *The World, the Text, and the Critic*. Cambridge: Harvard
    University Press, 1983. Print.
Saussy, Haun, Ed. *Comparative Literature in the Age of Globalization*.
    Baltimore, MD: Johns Hopkins University Press, 2006. Print.

Schütz, Anton. "Homo Sacer." In *The Agamben Dictionary*, Eds. Alex Murray and Jessica Whyte. Edinburgh: Edinburgh University Press, 2011. 94–96. Print.

Schwabsky, Barry. "Everyday Painting." In *Vitamin P2: New Perspectives in Painting*, Anon. Ed. New York: Phaidon Press, 2011. 10–16. Print.

Sedgwick, Eve Kosofsky. "Paranoid Reading and Reparative Reading, or, You're So Paranoid, You Probably Think This Essay Is about You." In *Touching Feeling: Affect, Pedagogy, Performativity*. Durham, NC: Duke University Press, 2003. 123–151. Print.

Shell, Marc and Werner Sollors, Eds. *Multilingual Anthology of American Literature: A Reader of Original Texts with English Translations*. New York: New York University Press, 2000. Print.

Sim, Stuart, Ed. *The Routledge Companion to Postmodernism*. 3rd ed. New York: Routledge, 2011. Print.

Smith, Paul, Ed. *Renewal of Cultural Studies*. Philadelphia, PA: Temple University Press, 2011. Print.

Sontag, Susan. "Against Interpretation." In *Against Interpretation and Other Essays*. New York: Picador, 2001. 3–14. Print.

Spivak, Gayatri Chakravorty. *In Other Words: Essays in Cultural Politics*. New York: Methuen, 1987. Print.

Stanford Literary Lab. http://litlab.stanford.edu. July 13, 2013.

Teres, Harvey. *The Word on the Street: Linking the Academy and the Common Reader*. Ann Arbor: University of Michigan Press, 2010. Print.

Towheed, Shafquat, Rosalind Crone, and Katie Halsey, Eds. *The History of Reading*. New York: Routledge, 2011. Print.

Turner, Graeme. *What's Become of Cultural Studies?* Los Angeles: Sage, 2012. Print.

Vizenor, Gerald. *Manifest Manners: Narratives on Postindian Survivance*. Middletown, CT: Wesleyan University Press, 1993. Print.

Wang, Ning. *Translated Modernities: Literary and Cultural Perspectives on Globalization and China*. New York: Legas, 2010. Print.

Warner, Michael. "Uncritical Reading." In *Polemic: Critical or Uncritical (Essays from the English Institute)*, Ed. Jane Gallop. New York: Routledge, 2004. 13–38. Print.

Weaver, Jace, Craig S. Womack, and Robert Warrior. *American Indian Literary Nationalism*. Albuquerque: University of New Mexico Press, 2006. Print.

Weinstein, Cindy and Christopher Looby, Eds. *American Literature's Aesthetic Dimensions*. New York: Columbia University Press, 2012. Print.

Wellek, René and Austin Warren. *Theory of Literature*. 3rd ed. New York: Harcourt Brace, 1962. Print.

Wiegman, Robyn. "The Vertigo of Critique." In *Object Lessons*. Durham, NC: Duke University Press, 2012. 301–343. Print.

Williams, Jeffrey J. "The Post-Welfare State University." *American Literary History* 18. Spring (2006): 190–216. Print.

———. "Prodigal Critics." *The Chronicle of Higher Education: The Chronicle Review* (December 6, 2009): B14–B15. Print.

———. "Deconstructing Academe: The Birth of Critical University Studies." *The Chronicle of Higher Education: The Chronicle Review* February 19, 2012. Web June 30, 2013.

——— and Heather Steffan, Eds. *The Critical Pulse: Thirty-Six Credos by Contemporary Critics*. New York: Columbia University Press, 2012. Print.

Williams, Raymond. *Culture and Society, 1780–1950*. London: Penguin, 1958. Print.

Womack, Craig S. *Red on Red: Native American Literary Separatism*. Minneapolis: University of Minnesota Press, 1999. Print.

Womack, Kenneth. "Selected Bibliography of Theory and Criticism." In *Norton Anthology of Theory and Criticism*. 2nd ed. Gen. Ed. Vincent B. Leitch. New York: W. W. Norton, 2010. 2655–2688. Print.

Woodmansee, Martha and Mark Osteen, Eds. *The New Economic Criticism: Studies at the Intersection of Literature and Economics*. New York: Routledge, 1999. Print.

Žižek, Slavoj. *The Sublime Object of Ideology*. The Essential Žižek Series. London: Verso, 2008. Print.

———. "Introduction: The Specter of Ideology." In *Mapping Ideology*. Ed. Slavoj Žižek. New York: Verso, 2012. 1–33. Print.

INDEX

Note: Locators followed by 'n' refer to notes.

Abrams, M. H. 11, 14, 15, 16
abstract expressionism 10
academic jobs ix, 10, 54, 72,
   144–6, 154–7
Adorno, Theodor W. 71
Agamben, Giorgio 139, 140, 142
All God's Chillun Got Wings
   (Eugene O'Neill) 47
Althusser, Louis x, 42, 43, 44n. 6,
   45, 109, 111
*American Indian Literary
   Nationalism* (Jace Weaver) 137
*American Literary Criticism from
   the 1930s to the 1980s* 2,
   26n. 5, 27n. 6, 82–3
Anderson, Amanda 20n. 4
animals 98, 101, 102
Antigone (Sophocles) 10
antitheory phenomenon 11–31,
   149
Armstrong, Paul B. 44n. 6
Aronowitz, Stanley 69
Auerbach, Erich 38

Badiou, Alain 91, 142, 143, 144
Balakrishnan, Gopal 134
Baron, Naomi S. 47n. 8
Bartolovich, Crystal 44n. 4
Bauerlein, Mark 20, 21, 22, 41
The Beast and the Sovereign
   (Jacques Derrida) 92–103
beat literature 10
bebop jazz 10

Belsey, Catherine 37n. 1
Berardi, Franco 145, 146
Bérubé, Michael 27n. 7
Best, Stephen 43, 44n. 6
Bewes, Timothy 44n. 6
big "T" Theory 28–31
Bleich, David 48
Bloom, Harold 14, 48, 113
blues festivals 85–6
Boltanski, Luc 45
Bóron, Atilio A. 134, 135n. 1
Boundary 2 group 1–2
Bourdieu, Pierre x, 60, 91, 109,
   111, 112, 113
Bousquet, Marc 144, 145, 146, 147
Brennan, Timothy 27n. 7
A Brief History of Neoliberalism
   (David Harvey) 140–2
Brooks, Cleanth 26, 38, 39, 40
Burke, Kenneth 26, 48
Butler, Judith 24, 44, 45, 48, 58,
   64, 65, 79

Caws, Mary Ann 38
"Charles Baudelaire's 'Les Chats'"
   (Roman Jakobson and
   Claude Lévi-Strauss) 38
Christian fundamentalism 6, 53
Circonfession (Jacques Derrida)
   114
close reading 38–41, 126–7
The Condition of Postmodernity
   (David Harvey) 140

contemporary academic labor
theory 145–6
corporate university xi, 3, 21–2,
25–6, 60, 72, 125, 127,
144–6, 149–50, 156
Corral, Will H. 11, 24, 31n. 9, 40
Cremaster Cycle (Matthew Barney)
68
*Critical Understanding: The
Powers and Limits of
Pluralism* (Wayne Booth) 22
critical university studies 127, 144
Culler, Jonathan 58
*Cultural Criticism, Literary Theory,
Poststructuralism* 1, 81–2
cultural critique 43–6, 83
cultural studies and theory vii, 54,
69–71, 75–7, 86
Culture and Imperialism (Edward
Said) 60
culture wars vii, 8, 12, 13n. 1, 18,
24, 40, 56, 149

Davis, Colin 48
Dean, Jodi 134
Debating Empire (Gopal
Balakrishnan) 134
"The Deconstructive Angel"
(M. H. Abrams) 14
Deconstructive Criticism 1–2
De Man, Paul 57, 60, 107, 108,
110, 112, 113, 118
de Manian deconstruction 15, 41n. 5
Derrickson, Teresa 146
Derrida (Benoît Peeters) 105–19
Derrida, Jacques
about family 106–7, 115
autobiographical writing 114
biography 105–6
critics and enemies 117
Derrida–Foucault quarrel
111–12
drug possession charges 107

friend/enemy basis 113
hermeticism and unreadability
117–18
philosophical disputes 111
politics of 107–8
relationship with
Bourdieu 112
French educational
institutions 109–10
Sylviana Agacinski 115–16
universities 110
Die Grundbegriffe der Metaphysik
(Martin Heidegger) 95
Discipline and Punish
(Michel Foucault) 65
Dissemination (Jacques Derrida) 59
distant reading 39n. 3
Does Literary Studies Have a Future
(Eugene Goodheart) 18
*Double Agent: The Critic and
Society* (Morris Dickstein)
16–17
DuBois, Andrew 38

Eagleton, Terry 20, 43
Ebert, Teresa 43
Eco, Umberto 77
Edmundson, Mark 36
egalitarianism 23, 45
Eliot, T. S. 47, 64, 79
Ellis, John M. 12, 13, 14, 40
Empire (Michael Hardt and
Antonio Negri) 65, 133–5
Empire and Imperialism
(Atilió Boron) 134
Empire's New Clothes (Paul
Passavant and Jodi Dean)
134
existentialism 10

Felski, Rita 36, 37
Female Masculinity
(Judith Halberstam) 65

Finnegans Wake (James Joyce) 15
For What Tomorrow
    (Jacques Derrida) 58
Foucault, Michel x, 2, 20, 36, 44,
    45, 64, 65, 91, 93, 94, 103,
    104, 105, 110, 111, 112,
    121, 139, 154
Foucaultian analysis 44
Franklin, Cynthia G. 105
Fraser, Nancy 138
Freedman, Diana P. 46
French theory 16, 24, 29, 56, 91–4
    future 103–4
Frey, Olivia 46
"Function of Criticism at the
    Present Time" (Matthew
    Arnold) 60–1
The Futures of American Studies 148

Gallop, Jane 41n. 5
gender demystification
    (Judith Butler) 44
Gender Trouble (Judith Butler) 65
Geneva phenomenology 44n. 6
Ginsberg, Benjamin 145
Gioia, Dana 40n. 4, 148
Goldstein, Philip 35
Goodheart, Eugene 18, 19, 20
Graff, Gerald 46
Graphs, Maps, Trees
    (Franco Moretti) 39n. 3
The Great Gatsby
    (F. Scott Fitzgerald) 47
Great Man and solitary genius
    theory 14
Groden, Michael 54

Hall, Stuart 9
Halsey, Katie 35
Hardt, Michael 44, 45, 65, 79, 88,
    128, 133, 134, 135, 139, 142
Harvey, David 9, 40n. 4, 140, 141,
    142, 147
Hassan, Ihab x, 124

Hayles, N. Katherine 60
Hebdige, Dick 79
Heidegger, Martin 6, 38, 57, 83,
    95, 96, 97, 98, 100, 102,
    107, 112, 139
heterogeneity 123
higher education and theory 151–7
"Historicization" 41n. 5
History of Sexuality
    (Michel Foucault) 65
Holbo, John 31n. 9
Holland, Norman 148
*Homo Sacer: Sovereign Power and
    Bare Life* (Giogio Agamben)
    139
hooks, bell 24, 63, 64, 65, 79
Hoover, Paul 128
*How the University Works:
    Higher Education and the
    Low-Wage Nation* (Marc
    Bousquet) 144–7
Hutcheon, Linda x, 126, 127

ideology critique 18–19, 41–3
incommensurability 123
individualism 23
Internet reading 47n. 8
intimate critique viii, 3, 45–6, 96,
    97, 136, 146
An Introduction to Arab Poetics
    (poet Adūnis) 79

Jackson, Michael, mediated death
    and burial of 74–7
Jacobs, Alan 46n. 7
Jacques, Martin 9
Jakobson, Roman 38
Jameson, Fredric 9, 20, 27, 43,
    44n. 6, 64, 65, 67, 121, 122
Jameson-style Marxist ideology
    critique 44n. 6
Jencks, Charles x, 124
Jenkins, Henry 34
Juhasz, Alexandra 47n. 8

Kantian antiutilitarian
    Enlightenment tradition 55
Keucheyan, Razmig 152

Lacan, Jacques x, 37n. 1, 91, 95,
    104
La Distinction (Pierre Bourdieu)
    112
"Language" (Martin Heidegger) 38
Latour, Bruno 38n. 2
late Derrida 58
Lentricchia, Frank 38
Lévi-Strauss, Claude 38, 79, 110
LGBTQ movements 44, 52, 148
life death theme 98–101
Lisse, Michel 93
literary criticism 17–19, 56
literature itself, concept 26, 54–5
*Literature Lost: Social Agendas
    and the Corruption of the
    Humanities* (John Ellis) 12
A Literature of Their Own
    (Elaine Showalter) 52
Living with Theory 9, 52, 67
Looby, Christopher 37n. 1

Machor, James L. 35
The Madwoman in the Attic
    (Sandra Gilbert and Susan
    Gubar) 52
Mallet, Marie-Louise 93
Marcus, Sharon 43, 44n. 6
Marxist-derived ideological
    analysis 41–43, 154
The Meaning of Sarkozy
    (Alain Badiou) 142–3
Michaels, Walter Benn 79, 138,
    139, 142, 147
Michaud, Ginette 93
Miller, J. Hillis 1, 14, 15, 16, 58
Mimesis (Erich Auerbach) 38
Moraru, Christian 127
Moretti, Franco 39n. 3, 60, 79, 148
multicultural theory 53

*Multilingual Anthology of
    American Literature: A
    Reader of Original Texts
    with English Translations*
    136

Natural Supernaturalism
    (M. H. Abrams) 14–15
Nealon, Jeffrey T. 124, 125, 126,
    127
Negri, Antonio 65, 79, 88, 133,
    134, 135n. 1, 139, 142
neoliberalism 2–4, 41–2, 57, 112,
    139–43, 154
neophenomenology 36–7, 44n. 6,
    48
New Age spirituality 6
New Critical formalism 1, 2, 7, 26,
    28, 39, 46, 54, 74
New World Order 63
Nietzschean-style genealogy 36
*Norton Anthology of Criticism and
    Theory* 7–8, 28, 30, 60–1,
    78–80, 131, 152

"Odysseus' Scar" (Erich Auerbach)
    38
Orientalism (Edward Said) 60, 65
Outlaw Culture (bell hooks) 65

paranoid reading 36
Passavant, Paul 134
Patai, Daphne 11, 24, 31n. 9,
    40
Pease, Donald E. 148
Peeters, Benoît x, 105, 106, 111,
    114, 115, 118, 119
Philosophy in a Time of Terror
    (Jacques Derrida) 58
"Plato's Pharmacy" (Jacques
    Derrida) 38
pleasure reading ix, 34–5
Poetics (Aristotle) 10
political correctness 13, 54

The Political Unconscious
    (Fredric Jameson) 65
post-Marxist cultural studies 1, 45
Postmodern American Poetry:
    A Norton Anthology
    (Paul Hoover) 128
postmodern culture features 67–8,
    77
postmodernism 9–10, 121–3
    case studies of 127–9
    concept 123–4
    critique of 130
    disorganization of culture 9, 129
    globalization 124
    phases 122
    post-postmodern 124–5
    rehistoricizing 129–30
    scholars of 123–4
    and theory 130–1
Postmodernism, or the Cultural
    Logic of Late Capitalism
    (Fredric Jameson) 65, 67–8,
    121
Postmodernism—Local Effects,
    Global Flows 7, 9
posttheory 16, 126, 130
"The Post-Welfare State
    University" (Jeffrey Williams)
    144n. 2
Pratt, Mary Louise 27
The Princeton Encyclopedia
    of Poetry and Poetics
    (Roland Greene) 127
psychoanalytic theory 37, 44, 97
public intellectual 108, 133, 142, 149
Pulitano, Elvira 137

Quicksand (Nella Larsen) 47

Radway, Janice 34, 35, 39, 40,
    47n. 8
Rancière, Jacques 38n. 2, 91
reading and textual interpretation
    94–7

Reading the Romance
    (Janice Radway) 35
Red on Red: Native American
    Literary Separatism
    (Craig Womack) 134–5
Reflections on Empire
    (Antonio Negri) 134
religion 6, 8–9, 68, 134–5, 148
Republic (Plato) 10
The Resisting Reader
    (Judith Fetterley) 52
resonance 61
Ricoeur, Paul 36, 109
Right to Sing the Blues
    (Jeff Melnick) 83
Robinson Crusoe (Daniel Defoe)
    95–6
Rogues (Jacques Derrida) 58
Roudinesco, Elisabeth 102
The Routledge Companion to
    Postmodernism (Stuart Sim)
    123
Rules of Art (Pierre Bourdieu) 60

Said, Edward W. 27, 60, 64, 65,
    79, 112
"Sarrasine," Balzac's story 38
School of Criticism and Theory 8,
    20n. 4
Schwabsky, Barry 128, 129
Sedgwick, Eve Kosofsky 20, 36,
    58, 79
Shell, Marc 136, 147
Sim, Stuart 123
social constructionism 20–1, 123
Sollors, Werner 136, 147
Sontag, Susan 36
Specters of Marx (Jacques Derrida)
    58, 96
Spivak, Gayatri Chakravorty 33,
    58, 79, 113, 153
Stanford Literary Lab 39n. 3
Story of Post-Modernism
    (Charles Jencks) 124

The Sublime Object of Ideology
(Slavoj Žižek) 65
The Sun Also Rises
(Ernest Hemingway) 47
survivance 99n. 1, 100
symptomatic reading 44n. 6

"Taboo and Critique: Literary
Criticism and Ethics" 1
Tel Quel journal 108
tenure system 21
theory 7, 29–30, 56–7, 68, 69,
130–1, 149–50, 152, 157
Theory Incorporated xi, 64, 70, 74,
151–2, 157
Theory of Literature (René Wellek
and Austin Warren) 12
Theory Market 154, 157
Theory Matters 9, 80–1, 84
*Theory's Empire: An Anthology
of Dissent* (Daphne Patai
and Will H. Corral) 11, 16,
27–30
*Toward a Native American Critical
Theory* (Elvira Pulitano) 137
tribalcentrism 147
*The Trouble with Diversity: How
We Learned to Love Identity
and Ignore Inequality*
(Walter Benn Michaels) 138–9
Turner, Graeme 54

Ulmer, Gregory 10

the Valve, literary Web blog 31n. 9
victimization thesis 45

Vitamin P (Barry Schwabsky in)
129
Vitamin P2 (Barry Schwabsky in)
129
Vizenor, Gerald 58, 99n. 1

Walten/walten 102
Warner, Michael 37, 38, 79
Warren, Austin 12
Warrior, Robert 137
The Waste Land (T. S. Eliot) 47
The Weary Blues
(Langston Hughes) 47
Weaver, Jace 137
Weinstein, Cindy 37n. 1
Wellek, René 11, 12, 82
The Well Wrought Urn
(Cleanth Brooks) 38
Western logocentrism 101
Wiegman, Robyn 45, 148
Williams, Jeffrey J. xi, 14, 144
Williams, Raymond 42
"Winter Evening" (Georg Trakl)
38
Womack, Craig S. 135, 136, 137,
138, 139, 142
The Worldly Philosophers
(Robert L. Heilbroner) 6
The Wretched of the Earth
(Frantz Fanon) 65
Wynema (Alice Callahan) 136

Yale deconstruction 1–2, 14–16

Zauhar, Frances Murphy 46
Žižek, Slavoj 43, 48, 60, 64, 65, 70